Praise for *Teach Happy*

Kim Strobel has perfectly created the formula of emotion + science + common sense to help educators love themselves and teaching again. *Teach Happy* is just what the doctor ordered! Kim offers practical resources for bringing joy back to education and also to your life. It's like you can hear her talking directly to you on every page. *Teach Happy* is the perfect guide to reclaiming your passion.

—**Steve Bollar,** educational thought leader, speaker, author, and consultant, Stand Tall Enterprises

Courageously vulnerable, powerfully authentic, and absolutely packed with practical ways to bring joy and happiness into your life, *Teach Happy* is a must-read for any educator navigating these tumultuous times. I don't currently have a life coach, but if I get one, it will be Kim Strobel.

—**Dave Burgess,** author of *Teach Like a Pirate*

Teach Happy is an empowering and actionable guide for educators looking to rediscover their passion and purpose, and to reclaim their profession and lives outside of it. Strobel combines personal insights with practical advice that is backed by science, offering a roadmap to happiness that feels both inspiring and achievable. If you are looking to infuse your work and life with genuine joy, this book is for you!

—**Lainie Rowell,** bestselling author, award-winning educator, and international keynote speaker

From her heart to yours. Buckle up and get ready to go on a journey of heart, soul, and instant application! We all could use more happiness in our lives, and Kim is bringing it to us!

—**LaVonna Roth,** Ignite Your S.H.I.N.E.®. Inc., keynote speaker and chief illuminator

Teach Happy

KIM STROBEL

TEACH HAPPY

Small Steps to BIG JOY

Teach Happy: Small Steps to Big Joy
© 2024 Kim Strobel

All rights reserved. No part of this publication may be reproduced in any form or by any electronic or mechanical means, including information storage and retrieval systems, without permission in writing by the publisher, except by a reviewer who may quote brief passages in a review. For information regarding permission, contact the publisher at books@impressbooks.org.

> This book is available at special discounts when purchased in quantity for educational purposes or for use as premiums, promotions, or fundraisers. For inquiries and details, contact the publisher at books@impressbooks.org.

Published by IMPress, a division of Dave Burgess Consulting, Inc.
IMPressbooks.org
DaveBurgessConsulting.com
San Diego, CA

Paperback ISBN: 978-1-948334-71-6
Ebook ISBN: 978-1-948334-72-3

Cover and interior design by Liz Schreiter
Edited and produced by Reading List Editorial
ReadingListEditorial.com

To my husband, Scott. For the last seven years, I've told you, "I'm going to write a book." Each time, you believed me. Babe, I finally did it.

Also, to all the educators and students who have impacted me along the way. Your stories of vulnerability and struggle have inspired me to show up for you and make education a better place.

CONTENTS

Preface 1
Chapter 1: From Panic to Purpose 9
Chapter 2: The Happy Teacher Equation 19
Chapter 3: Keeping It Real 30
Chapter 4: Redefining Happiness 39
Chapter 5: The Art of Flow 47
Chapter 6: Words Have Power 59
Chapter 7: Exercise Drives Happiness 69
Chapter 8: The Aligned Heart 78
Chapter 9: Minimum Effective Dose 87
Chapter 10: Radical Wellness 95
Chapter 11: You're Worth It 107
Chapter 12: The Magic of Play 117
Chapter 13: The Ripple of Hope 124

Bibliography 129
Endnotes 131
Acknowledgments 136
About the Author 138
More from IMPress 142

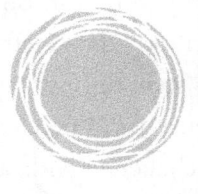

PREFACE

Remember Your Why: Corey

As a young teacher, I was a connoisseur of all things inspirational. My desk was adorned with framed quotes like "A teacher's influence never ends" and good old Thoreau's "Go confidently in the direction of your dreams! Live the life you've imagined." I went into teaching because I believed in these corny quotes and in my capacity to influence students' lives.

In those early, idealistic years as a young teacher, I was very focused on teaching academics. I knew my students needed to learn their curricular standards in order to pass state tests, and I would do whatever it took to help them learn and achieve. But with all of the pressure I put on myself, I also felt completely overwhelmed. It was easy for me to get lost in the fray of everything I was supposed to be doing: teaching academic standards, differentiating instruction, making learning exciting, analyzing data, adjusting or creating lessons, changing the bulletin board, integrating technology, composing the weekly newsletter, and responding to the avalanche of emails in my inbox.

Faced with this deluge of tasks, I looked at my happy desk quotes and soldiered on. As a classic type A personality, I would walk out the glass doors of my school each afternoon to go home only after every single item was ticked off my to-do list. But even though I was keeping up with my tasks, there were still days I left feeling like I wasn't enough. Maybe my writing lessons were top-notch one week, but I completely let social studies slip because I didn't have enough time. Or maybe I mishandled a behavioral challenge with a student. Maybe I lost my patience with my class. I walked out those doors with my head hung low at times, feeling like I had been defeated once again, disappointing not just myself but even old, dead Henry David Thoreau.

Educators face incredible pressures, which can lead to burnout. As a result, it's critical for us to maintain perspective on the deeper impacts of our work and to hold on to empathy—both for our students and ourselves. Luckily, even as I was setting unattainable expectations for myself, I met a student who helped me to maintain that perspective.

In my seventh year of teaching fourth grade, I met Corey. According to his previous teachers, he was the kind of kid every educator should be afraid to see on their class roster. And there he was on mine. His name practically jumped off the page and into my psyche.

Corey came into my class like a Tasmanian devil on fire. Each morning, he entered the room empty-handed, smelling like a smokestack. There was always a zero-percent chance his homework was complete or that any papers had been signed by his parents. He spent his days zipping around the classroom, fidgeting at his desk, and prodding other students. He did everything possible to derail my teaching. Even the other students in the class grew frustrated with Corey and his distractions.

From the time Corey entered my classroom, I was determined not to let his interruptions faze me. I remembered a book I had read in my first year of teaching about building relationships, so I was lucky enough to know how important relationships and classroom climate are in creating a caring and happy learning environment. So, even when he was driving me crazy, I put on a smile and did my best to greet him each morning with a high five and a "Good morning, Corey, come on in!" I cared deeply for him, but in my head, each day, I would think, "How am I going to maintain control with him again today?"

Keeping in mind the book I'd read about classroom climate, I began implementing one of the strategies I'd learned: a fifteen-minute classroom meeting after lunch each day. This became an important part of my classroom structure. When students came in after lunch, we gathered in a circle to meditate. Of course, twenty years ago, I didn't call it meditating—that would have been labeled as too unconventional. So, I think I called this activity classroom meeting time.

To perform this meeting time, students sat comfortably on the floor and held their pinky, index, and middle fingers together on each hand while concentrating on their breathing. We would do this for two to three minutes. Then we would go around the room, and each child would share one of three things:

1. A gratitude—something they were thankful for that day.
2. An appreciation—a compliment to someone who did something nice that day.
3. A struggle—something hard in their lives.

While I felt this classroom meeting practice was important and created a safe space filled with kindness, well-being, and vulnerability, I did not expect it to teach me the biggest lesson of my teaching career.

On a cold day in the winter of that year, we gathered on the floor for our meeting. Most students chose to share something they were grateful for or an appreciation, but when it was Corey's turn to share, his eyes glistened with tears, and he said, "I want to share a struggle today." The room fell quiet, and my breath caught as he continued talking. "My mom is in jail," he told us. "She's got an alcohol problem. I'm afraid to leave school today because I don't know where I'll go. I don't have a dad in my life."

Corey bravely told us these intimate, brutal details of his life. Later, I learned that it was even more bleak than he told the class. His mother wasn't giving him his ADD medicine because she stayed in her room day and night. He was scared to leave school on Fridays because there was little food in the house on the weekends, and he didn't have heat in the trailer where he lived.

On that day, my entire perspective on teaching changed, and I believe Corey's story changed my other twenty-seven students too. It was like the air literally transformed in the classroom when Corey spoke. The other students' faces softened, and we saw Corey in a whole new way. This shift in the class's relationship to Corey was empathy personified.

As the weeks progressed, I noticed how my students embraced Corey for who he was while also learning to be more supportive of him. Two of my students, Jackson and Chandler, told Corey that they noticed math was especially stressful for him, and they offered to be his math tutors. They told him that whenever he got stuck, he could come and ask them for help. It was a delight to see Corey walk over to Chandler's desk and to watch the three boys work together.

Two girls in my class said, "Hey, Corey, we'd like to help you at the end of the day so you can get organized and take any papers home with you." Each afternoon, they'd go to Corey's disheveled desk and help him write down items in his agenda for the next day and ensure he had his homework and books in his backpack. The students even befriended Corey and, instead of rolling their eyes at him, they started to include him in games and activities.

I'm embarrassed to admit that before Corey shared his struggles with us, I would have him sit on the curb at recess and do his late homework. I thought the best way to help him was to make sure he caught up in school, but I was missing the root of his problems. Corey didn't have a supportive adult at home to help him understand the importance of learning. He didn't have anyone to help him with his homework. He was worried about his mother, staying warm at night, and whether or not he'd have food to eat. When the students and I started to embrace Corey for who he was, everything changed.

Corey provided me with one of the most valuable teaching moments of my time as an educator. In fact, I believe the trajectory of my teaching career totally changed when I realized he was a misunderstood and deeply wounded boy. From that moment on, I restructured and changed everything when it came to how I dealt with Corey. I never again penalized him for not having his homework done; he needed to experience the fun of socializing and playing with friends. I learned to extend much more grace to Corey because I finally understood the story that came with the boy.

As I empathized with Corey emotionally, I also found ways to support him pragmatically. Corey began meeting with our caring school counselor, Sally, who helped him navigate some tough situations. Our school food backpack program sent food home with Corey on the weekends, and I was able to find him a Big Brother who was a tremendous, continual support in his life for years going forward. Once he had the support he needed, Corey began to care more about learning. He went from being disruptive to a happy and cooperative kid. He simply came alive in our classroom, and it was a remarkable thing to witness.

Five weeks before school was out that year, I discovered a note on my desk at the end of the day. Here are a few sentences from it:

> *This year has been spectacular. I will miss you. You have been the best teacher ever. You have taught me that school is important. I don't want the school year to end. I will be crying. I will be thinking about you. I did not like school, and now I love school. I have never been a writer, and now I'm a good writer. Just look at how long this letter is. Everyone in class is a family and a good family. Every time I get my homework done, they give me a high five. No one has ever done that for me. No one used to like me, and now they do because of you. Thank you so much.*

It was apparent that our schoolroom had become Corey's safe haven, and we had become his family. He felt safe. He felt loved. He felt valued. This letter is one of my most prized possessions. Sometime later, I turned the letter over, and there was an angel on the back of it, under which he had written "Mrs. Strobel."

I have continued to stay in contact with Corey over the years. For a time, his life continued down a dark road. I heard Corey's mother died of an overdose, so he was sent to live in a different city with an alcoholic and emotionally abusive dad who had never been in his life. A few years later, when I became the curriculum director in the same city to which Corey had moved, I continued to check in with him. Against all odds, Corey had grown into an A/B student. To this day, he has continued on a trajectory of success despite the obstacles he has faced.

I continue to follow Corey's journey as an integral part of his life. I've witnessed some profound moments of tremendous pride and gratitude for Corey. In May of 2022, I sat in the bleachers at the University of Southern Indiana and watched Corey walk across the stage to receive his bachelor's degree in health sciences. In August of 2022, I sat in a church pew and watched Corey stand at the front of the altar fighting off tears of happiness as his high school sweetheart made her way down the aisle to become his wife. Corey has overcome so much and has much to contribute to this world. I cannot wait to see what he accomplishes.

Corey still sends me messages from time to time, and they always say things like this:

> *God put you in my life for a very special reason. I know I was only in fourth grade and didn't know a thing about the world. But it was a turning point in my life. I'm sure most people who knew me back then thought I wouldn't amount to much and I would just end up a statistic. You believed in me when I'm sure very little did, and you changed my life in that fourth-grade classroom. I've had plenty of people help me out and support me throughout the years, but no one quite like you. If not for you believing in me at a young age, I could have easily gone down*

a destructive path that led to nothing. I can't thank you enough for all you've done. You changed my life.

Corey's transformation wasn't just the result of my intervention or Corey's own efforts; it was enabled by an entire community. Corey was lucky enough to have other teachers along the way who knew the value of relationships and looked at students as people instead of grades. They, too, have contributed to his success.

I look back to that fourth-grade year with Corey in 2009. I thought I was going to be Corey's teacher, but he ended up being mine. Corey taught me that before we can even begin teaching our students math or reading, we must first teach them that they are loved and valued. This message seems obvious, but the current education system has placed so many other requirements and standards on us that it's easy to forget.

To this day, Corey also influences how I show up for teachers and how I want to help them impact and influence the students they teach. Corey transformed my career by giving me the drive, as my friend Henry would say, to help teachers "live the lives they've imagined."

As a continuation of that project, my goal for this book is for each of you to take a step back from work, grades, and evaluations and start thinking about the deeper impact that we, as educators, can have on our students and the impact they can have on us. A lot of us have trauma, just like Corey, that we carry with us into the classroom, and that trauma compounds the burnout we may already feel as we grapple with the increasing lists of demands that are placed on us.

As you read on, then, I hope that you will realize it might be time for you to own your struggles and to start adjusting your own life. As teachers, we care deeply about our students, and Corey's story demonstrates that students need to feel seen, heard, valued, and loved. But guess what? So do teachers.

As teachers, we may feel invisible as we work endlessly to help students become successful. But we all deserve to live lives that feel good to us a lot of the time; we all deserve to feel happy as teachers, even if the vocation of teaching makes happiness feel hard. Despite those challenges, I know from years of struggling that success as an educator comes only when we nourish our emotional well-being. Only when we begin to heal and nurture our soul can we start to show up as our best selves for our students.

We deserve to have space and ease as we go along this journey of teaching—and as we live out the equally important other parts of our lives. We may need some grace to learn that we matter, too, but my hope is that the science, strategies, and tools in this book will help you learn how to reach and capture more happiness along the way.

From the rooftops, we shout, "Kids deserve your very best!" While I believe this to be true, you can't show up as your best self if you're constantly depleted and unable to care for your needs outside of this demanding career. You, too, deserve to feel seen, heard, valued, and loved. I hope that this book does that for you.

Chapter 1

FROM PANIC TO PURPOSE

My Journey to Becoming a Happiness Coach

Sometimes, when I get introduced to a crowd as a former teacher and a curriculum director who's now a *happiness coach*, I feel like people expect a shiny unicorn with pink cotton candy hair to walk out onstage.

When I'm standing behind the curtain, waiting to greet the audience, I often imagine what the people in the crowd are thinking.

"A happiness coach? Get real!"

"Oh, good grief, someone who's happy all the time."

"This must be a joke."

But I'm quick to let the crowd know that becoming a happiness coach resulted from my own struggles and trauma, as well as years of intense and silent suffering. Because of my difficult past, I believe I was meant to become a teacher first and then a happiness coach, even if I had to go through a lot of dark times to get here. My work as a happiness coach may surprise audiences, but it may strike people who have known me a long time, or who know me very well, as deeply ironic.

In fact, I've pretty much been a nervous Nellie since I was a little girl. In elementary school, I worried about my older brothers a lot. In the evenings I would race outside to look for my brothers, who were usually playing around the neighborhood. If they weren't in sight, I'd convince myself that they'd been kidnapped and begin searching for them frantically.

That anxiety carried over to what should have been joyful experiences. When I was in the fifth grade, my parents surprised me and my siblings with a trip to Disney World. While my brothers jumped up and down with excitement, I sat paralyzed, thinking of all the things that could go wrong on the trip. "What if my brothers get lost in the park?" I worried to myself. "What if someone steals them away? What if they leave me forever?"

So, I told my parents the only way I would go to Disney World was if I could have one of those leash systems attached to my wrist and the other two ends attached to my brothers' wrists. Even though my parents were incredibly responsible, I still felt like I was the only one who could keep my brothers safe. My mother recognized that this wasn't normal eleven-year-old behavior and decided to take me to counseling. I went to a few sessions and they helped for a while, but my anxiety persisted.

In middle school, I started experiencing obsessive-compulsive tendencies. Each morning I would stand in the bathroom and look at the plug to my curling iron multiple times while I got ready for school, convincing myself it was unplugged. Then I would walk down the hallway to the kitchen for breakfast and tell myself that if I didn't touch the hallway wall in a certain place, something bad would happen to my family that day.

These rules I set for myself were cumbersome and sucked the energy out of me. On top of that, I felt guilty for having obsessive thoughts in the first place, because my brain knew my rules were irrational.

But the behavior grew more elaborate. I became convinced that if my dad didn't get home from work at 6:00 p.m. on the dot, he had died in a car accident on his way home. Every night I paid close attention to the clock, and if Dad wasn't home by 5:50 p.m., I'd start to get nauseous. If ten minutes passed and he still hadn't arrived, I'd go to the bathroom and sit on the cold tile floor, thinking I might be sick. By the time he walked through the door, I would be so riddled with fear that I'd be shaking.

My parents' answer to this problem was to make sure my dad started coming home at 5:50 p.m. so I wouldn't worry. But my fears simply outsmarted this attempt at a solution: my worrying routine moved up to 5:45 p.m.

Believe it or not, I was a so-called normal child. I had lots of friends, did well in sports, and was even voted homecoming queen by my classmates. By the time I entered high school, I felt like I was coming into myself: the high school version of me was new, improved, and full of confidence. I was strong, had an exuberant personality, had lots of friends, and was having loads of fun in high school.

But then, during my sophomore year, out of nowhere, I started having terrible episodes. One day while sitting at my desk in the middle of language arts class, the room got hot and the walls felt like they were caving in, as if the whole classroom were growing smaller. Everything looked blurry and disorienting. I suddenly felt like I was going to pass out. My whole body shook as I overheated. Somehow, in that God-awful state, I was able to tell the teacher that I felt ill, and I escaped to the nurse's office.

As an adult, I have a framework for understanding these episodes: they were panic attacks. But as a child, I had no words for what was happening to me; I only had the experiences themselves. For readers who have never had a panic attack, I want to thoroughly explain what one feels like to me.

Imagine you're standing on a train track facing an oncoming train. Even though the train is traveling toward you at three hundred miles per hour, your feet are chained to the track and you are not able to move. The train will stop one inch before it hits you. Those few minutes, while you stand on the tracks with the train barreling toward you, will be excruciating. Your heart will start pumping like it's going to jump out of your chest, and your entire body will shake uncontrollably. You will feel like you're balancing between consciousness and unconsciousness and that, at any second, you might faint.

Everything around you will look blurry, contorted, and confusing. You might even feel like you're having an out-of-body experience. So, even as the train rushes toward you, you begin to feel disconnected from your environment and the people around you. You will feel strange and like you are about to lose complete control and any connection to everything around you.

But the reality of panic attacks is that there is no train! You are 100 percent safe. You will not be harmed. You are not in danger. I promise the train won't hit you.

For me, these attacks would come out of nowhere. My brain couldn't find a logical reason for my symptoms, and because of that, I felt like I was going crazy. These episodes kept happening, and I had no idea why. The uncertainty of the onset of these irrational feelings forced me to constantly monitor my bodily and mental sensations. I felt completely unsafe in my school, home, and body. The situation got worse and worse until I was having multiple episodes a day.

Noticing these episodes, my mom took me to a doctor, who decided I had low blood sugar and recommended I start a new diet. So, I avoided sugar like the plague and made sure to eat every two hours just like the doctor told me to. But, despite the ease of the doctor's assessment, the attacks continued.

So, my mom took me to a neurologist, who diagnosed me with complex partial seizures. He put me on Depakote, which seemed to reduce the number of episodes I was having, but it didn't take away the fear that I could have one at any moment. Years later, I discovered that Depakote is also an anxiety reducer, but it's not the preferred one for my particular disorder. Because, as it turns out, I was misdiagnosed again.

My panic attacks were frustratingly unpredictable, which made it impossible to live the life I wanted. Things would get slightly better, but then the episodes would start back up again, worse than ever before. I completely lost myself for almost ten years, from age sixteen to about twenty-four.

At that point, I was having multiple attacks per day, which made even mundane tasks impossible. I struggled to drive anywhere, go into a Walmart, walk around the block, or even go get my mail. Driving five minutes to the secretarial job I had in college felt like the world's hardest task. Things became so bad that I had to quit college because I was afraid to be away from my home and my parents.

My panic attacks thus led to a period of extreme darkness and suffering in my life. I felt like I had an inner spirit that was full of life, vibrancy, and confidence, and then all of a sudden, I was plagued by panic disorder. So, the real Kim inside me was completely stonewalled by a psychological limitation. I felt lost, inadequate, and helpless. I also struggled silently with my panic attacks because I was so ashamed of them. Every five minutes of every day was a struggle because I never knew when I'd feel the train charging toward me. I started to fear my fear, which became an endless cycle of suffering.

I was broken, beaten down, and exhausted from living my life, but I also developed coping strategies. I created what I considered "safe" people in my life: my mom and my husband. These were people who knew my dirty, dark secrets. They were the people I could run to if I had an episode.

While these loved ones provided a sense of security, my strategy had a drawback: I completely alienated myself from anything in my life that didn't feel safe. As a result, I became agoraphobic, afraid to leave the house, be left alone, drive my car, walk inside a mall, or go to the supermarket. The shame and complete loss of any self-confidence was devastating.

Finally, things came to an all-time low. My husband at the time would leave for work twenty minutes earlier than me. For those twenty minutes, I would be so nervous that I would have a panic attack, but I wouldn't be able to get help because I was alone. With no other options for safety, I'd grab the phone only to convince myself not to call 911. When the fear subsided, I'd force myself to go back into the bathroom and continue getting ready for work—but then the feelings would return and I'd run back to the phone, ready to call for help.

On one particular morning when I found myself, for the hundredth time, standing next to the phone with the receiver in hand and my fingers ready to dial 911, I dropped the phone, closed myself in the bathroom, and curled up in the fetal position on my bath mat. Still, to this day, I get emotional thinking about this moment. I remember every detail about it. I vividly remember lying on the forest-green bath mat and feeling my cheek against its plushness.

I lay there on the floor and pleaded to God. It makes me sad to say, but I was begging Him to take my life. I couldn't bear to take my own life, and honestly I wanted to live, but I didn't know how to keep living in a constant state of distress. So, I just needed Him to intervene and end my life for me. I didn't know how to fix myself. I needed relief, and death felt like the answer.

But, after a few minutes of lying on the floor, I heard a message. Even now, I don't know if I heard a voice or if it was inner knowing from the depths of my soul, but I heard "Kim, you are made for more. Get off that bath mat and let's get some help. You are made for more than this." It makes me tear up when I think about being a helpless young woman fighting to just feel normal.

Shortly after that, somehow, I ended up at my primary physician's office. Dr. Ress had an interest in the new findings about anxiety disorders. I will never forget when he looked me in the eyes and said, "Kim, I believe you have what is called 'panic disorder.' This means that there is a chemical imbalance in your brain that is causing you to feel this way. The chemicals are called neurotransmitters or serotonin, but we have medicine that can help with this."

I can't tell you the relief I felt. For years, I had been suffering from a condition I didn't have a name for and didn't know how to treat. There were times I didn't think I'd ever be able to live a normal life. Dr. Ress wrote me a prescription for Zoloft, and that medication, along with other important supports, completely changed my life. I went from having multiple panic attacks daily to having none in about two months.

Dr. Ress also suggested counseling, so I went to a psychologist, who did months of cognitive behavioral therapy with me. In therapy I had to challenge my terror-filled thoughts and try to learn that I was safe and that I wasn't in any real danger. I also had to practice exposure therapy, meaning I had to force myself to experience things I found terribly scary.

For me just going to the grocery store was terrifying. So, my homework was to drive to Walmart, go inside, walk to the back wall, and touch it—then I could leave. I had to do this daily for weeks. The sensations I was most afraid of were dizziness, unreality, and feeling faint. Thankfully, at that time I worked as a secretary at the prosecutor's office, and everyone left for lunch. So, I would go into my boss's office and sit in his desk chair and force myself to spin round and round so I could teach my brain that I could feel disoriented while remaining safe.

After I was prescribed the right medicine, practiced extensive cognitive behavioral therapy, and found other practices, I discovered the self-help field. And let me tell you, I was on fire with it. I read every self-help book I could get my hands on. They fed my soul in a way that it had never been fed, and I continue to immerse myself in self-help literature today. I also read books that helped me understand more about panic and agoraphobia and what was happening in my brain.

Armed with these resources, I was determined to take 100 percent responsibility for my life, and I was playing to win. I was doing every exercise I could to retrain my brain. I was reading any book I could about improving myself. I was on a mission to reclaim my life.

Thanks to my self-help journey, I started to rebuild my life and got myself back to college even while I was still having panic attacks. With renewed momentum around my career, I grew determined to obtain my teaching degree. Thanks to a supportive boss, I was able to work full-time while going to classes full-time, and so I made that dream a reality.

Once I landed a job as an educator, I adored teaching kids. Most days, I loved showing up for my students, knowing I had the grand opportunity to impact and influence their lives.

And all the while, I continued to work on myself. I started to reclaim the deepest parts of who I was and how I wanted to show up in the world. The fire in my belly was lit, and my confidence grew. My inner desires to lead, empower, and make a positive impact on the world and others around me became stronger and stronger. I could say yes to going somewhere by myself, getting on a plane and traveling solo, or simply walking in Walmart. I didn't have to live with a smaller version of myself that wasn't aligned to how I wanted to show up for life.

Teaching and Unhappiness

I start with my own story of struggle and self-help because it is the foundation of who I am and what I do. I am a woman who can be fierce on the stage and empower others, but I am also a woman who still has challenges. I've been learning to embrace both parts of me.

After years of practicing all the methods I'd learned from therapists and in books, I finally felt like I had my life back, even though the struggle can still be real at times. When I was in a place where I could look back on those dark times, I started to think about all the people who were out there and still struggling. I knew I needed to share my journey and my knowledge with the world. And this, my friends, is the very long story of how I became a happiness coach.

As a happiness coach, I work with thousands of teachers all across the country. As educators, we serve in one of the most stress-filled, heavyhearted professions out there. Every single one of us has struggled, suffered, and endured some type of darkness or had painful things happen in our lives. In my work, I meet so many teachers who are suffering from anxiety, stress, guilt, and feelings of defeat. In fact, when Dr. Ress treated me, he said, "Kim, the number one reason I see patients is for the common cold. The number two reason is to treat anxiety, and the number one client group who come for this help . . . are schoolteachers."

I've spoken to thousands of teachers who are suffering under the workload of this profession and what it demands. One of my favorite things after I give a keynote is to spend time connecting with teachers. Many times, they find me at the front of the room and embrace me in tears. They speak about feeling called to be in this profession, but they're wondering what they can possibly "let go of" to reclaim some peace in the other parts of their life. These teachers are full of heart, but what they are enduring feels unbearable at times. They are sad, anxious, and depressed, feeling like they simply can't get their head above water.

As Jennifer, an elementary teacher, recently said to me, "I feel like teaching carries an emotional toll not experienced in most other careers, and you can't turn it off. You constantly worry about your students, their safety, their learning and emotional states. Every week there seems to be an addition to your responsibilities, but no more time to complete them. Everyone is stretched thin, and we often have to cover for each other, losing what little prep time we have. If you do prioritize yourself or your family, it feels as if you're being selfish."

Kristen, an eighth-grade ELA teacher, told me, "Kim, just today I was wrestling with the need to teach my next class with the need to immediately report the concerning behaviors of my previous class.

Do I neglect one class of thirty students to report the nonemergency bad behaviors of students, or do I neglect to report the bad behavior until I have time to breathe, which would be after I do my after-school tutoring for kids who are struggling? I feel like nothing gets done well, the stress builds, and I've failed once again."

I do not want to diminish the hard or real pain these educators are feeling. This profession is out of control, and it seems no one has answers for how they can get their sanity back. But that is what this book does. This book helps teachers not be enslaved to a system and instead take control of the only thing that is in their control: how they operate in this system.

But while I know, based on my own experiences in and out of the classroom, that this profession is incredibly hard, I also know we can rise above those challenges. Toward that end, the goal of this book is to help educators find our way to the light so that we can show up to serve in a profession that is so full of heart that, at times, it steals from other parts of our lives.

This book is about embracing the parts of us that struggle while owning our worth in this world. And, in that sense, it's ultimately about happiness. My journey from darkness to light led me to become a happiness coach and to share my story with you. I learned skills that changed my life, and now I want to help others learn skills to improve their own well-being. Together, we can reclaim our profession and our lives outside of it.

Chapter 2

THE HAPPY TEACHER EQUATION

Understanding Contributors to Happiness

Happy people don't just sit around being content. One study observed genuinely happy people and found that they make things happen.[1] Happy people have a vision for their life; they seek new lessons and achievements. They are intentional with their thoughts, actions, and behaviors. They establish daily happiness habits that are a part of their everyday lives. It's important to understand the relevant research about happiness because knowledge is power. In the coming chapters, we'll talk about how to turn knowledge into action, which is real power.

Positive psychology has been extensively established as a field of study by many social scientists over the last forty years, most notably by Martin Seligman, the director of the Positive Psychology Center at the University of Pennsylvania, and by Shawn Achor, who taught the first positive psychology class at Harvard.

Positive psychology's insights aren't just limited to academic inquiry, though. According to the Positive Psychology Institute, "Positive Psychology is the scientific study of human flourishing, and an applied approach to optimal functioning. It has also been defined as the study of the strengths and virtues that enable individuals, communities, and organizations to thrive."[2] The field is thus founded on the belief that people want to lead meaningful and fulfilling lives.

In some ways, positive psychology is the study of how people learn to thrive. Achor notes that "the typical approach to understanding human behavior has always been to look for the average behavior or outcome."[3] For his research, though, Achor chose to study the outliers by asking several key questions: "Why is it that some people are so ahead of the curve when it comes to how they deal with stress in the face of challenges? Why are they more creative and able to see possibilities where others see defeat? Why are they more energetic, vibrant, happier, and engaged in life, and what are they doing differently than the average?" Thanks to positive psychology, we are beginning to find answers to these mysteries.[4]

In my opinion and from what I've learned, I believe that positive psychology, happiness, and well-being are interwoven terms when it comes to understanding what happiness is—because it's so hard to define. Is it a feeling? A state? Do we arrive there? I don't think it's any of these. In fact, I don't think it's a destination. Arthur Brooks, who teaches happiness courses at Harvard University, says, "Happiness is a direction. We won't find complete happiness on this side of heaven, but no matter where each of us is in life, we can all be happier."[5] I've learned a lot from Brooks in his book *Build the Life You Want*. He explains that we can be a mixture of happy and unhappy at the same time.[6] Happiness doesn't come only after you've rid yourself of all your unhappiness. For example, today I was super happy when I woke up because our son is home from Boston. Then, I opened my email and saw that we were behind on a project because we had some snafus. My stress level immediately climbed. Then I trotted into the kitchen to grab some chocolate chip cookies to make myself feel better and my happiness climbed for about two minutes. Then I felt guilty because I ate the darn cookies. But then I went for a run with my dogs and I was all happy again.

Brooks also explains, "We can also stop believing that our individual problems are the reasons we haven't achieved happiness. No positive circumstance can give us the state of bliss we seek. But no negative circumstance can make getting happier impossible."[7] Brooks believes that happiness has three major ingredients: enjoyment, satisfaction, and purpose. So, I believe happiness is how much of those three ingredients we feel in our lives and how we can feel more of them.

As you'll learn in this book, regardless of our life experiences, our hardships, the roughness and toughness of life in general, we can all get happier.

Because it is concerned with emotions and experiences, positive psychology can sometimes feel abstract; however, its lessons are often deeply personal in their impacts. Before we can get started on improving our happiness, it's important to reflect and evaluate where we are in our happiness journey. To start, I want to ask you one question:

What would make you happier?

Take some time to reflect on what you think would contribute to your happiness. For now, just remember your answers. We will talk in depth in this chapter about the factors that actually go into making us happy. When we discover this, we cultivate the ability to create our happiness within ourselves, thereby shifting the lever in every other part of our lives.

Once you're done, I recommend this quiz, *The Authentic Happiness Inventory*, created by the aforementioned Dr. Martin Seligman. After completing the questionnaire, you will receive results that will give you a snapshot of how potentially happy you are with your life. You can find the quiz at the QR code:

Happiness Research

I first discovered happiness research while reading Sonja Lyubomirsky's book *The How of Happiness*. According to Lyubomirsky, each of us is born with a baseline happiness level, a so-called set point.[8] This set point is similar to the way our bodies gravitate toward a certain weight: some of us are born with skinny genes and can eat McDonald's french fries and not gain a pound, while some of us might diet for months only to gain the weight right back. So, when good things happen in our lives—like when we buy a house, get married, or just go shopping for the day—our happiness levels go up. We might experience this increase for two minutes or two years, but eventually, our happiness will level out and we will return to our genetic set point, our baseline of happiness. The human ability to adjust to feelings that we experience is called hedonic adaptation.

That "reset" for happiness might be disappointing, but thankfully research says that the inverse is also true. So, it's been proved that humans can endure heartache, loss, illness, adversity, challenges, and injustices and still return to their baseline happiness levels. For example, studies conducted on people with renal disease showed that despite having intense weekly dialysis sessions and dealing with a multitude of symptoms, those subjects were still as happy as the control group of healthy participants. As Lyubomirsky states, "Amazing as it may seem, people show a great deal of adaptation to disabilities like paralysis and blindness and other conditions that involve losing an important capacity or function."[9]

Teachers have to adapt all the time. I know many teachers who started off teaching classes of twenty kids, and that was considered a full class. The next year they added a few more kids to the class, and at first, it was hard, but they quickly adapted to twenty-two kids. The next year the same thing happened until they were teaching a classroom of thirty kids without questioning whether they could do it or not.

I once knew a teacher who lost her mother at the beginning of the year. They were extremely close, and for a while, it was difficult for this teacher to imagine how she could ever be happy again. Each day she came in and taught her students, but she was still struggling mentally. By the end of the year, when I asked her how she was doing, there was a sparkle in her eyes again. While she still missed her mother, she had been able to work through her grief and return to her baseline of happiness. This is not to say that she didn't still experience grief, but she was able to continue moving forward in her life.

Hedonic adaptation is further illustrated in the book *Man's Search for Meaning* by Viktor Frankl. During the Holocaust, Frankl was sent to four concentration camps over the course of three years. His father and brother both died at camps, his mother died at Auschwitz, and his wife, Tilly, starved to death in the women's camp at Bergen-Belsen.[10] Despite enduring indescribable suffering, Frankl went on to live a joyful and meaningful life. In his book, he talks about how he had so much taken from him, but he knew no one could take away his thoughts, nor could they take away his hope. Famously, Frankl reflected on his experiences by writing, "The one thing you can't take away from me is the way I choose to respond to what you do to me. The last of one's freedoms is to choose one's attitude in any given circumstance. Happiness cannot be pursued; it must ensue. Life is never made unbearable by circumstances, but only by lack of meaning and purpose."[11] Stories like Frankl's, and research on hedonic adaptation, show that humans are resilient. We can endure unimaginable suffering and have the capacity to return to our baseline happiness.

Still, when I read stories like Frankl's, it's hard for me to imagine being as strong and resilient in the face of extreme loss as Frankl was. Then I think about the people I know who have experienced horrific tragedies and still live happy lives. A friend of mine endured date rape, an abusive marriage, two miscarriages, divorce, bankruptcy, and four fights with cancer, and still, when asked about her life, she says, "God is good and my life is full of joy and laughter and meaning." I think about all the others I have seen who have survived hard things, and most live good, happy lives. I bet you know some of these people too.

Breaking Down Happiness

Lyubomirsky's insights into positive psychology aren't limited to explaining how happiness operates; they also help to explain what happiness is. So, beyond suggesting that all humans possess a baseline happiness, Lyubomirsky has found that our happiness is the result of three major sources: genetics; circumstances; and thoughts, actions, and behaviors.[12] I like to think of happiness as a pie chart divided into three different sections.

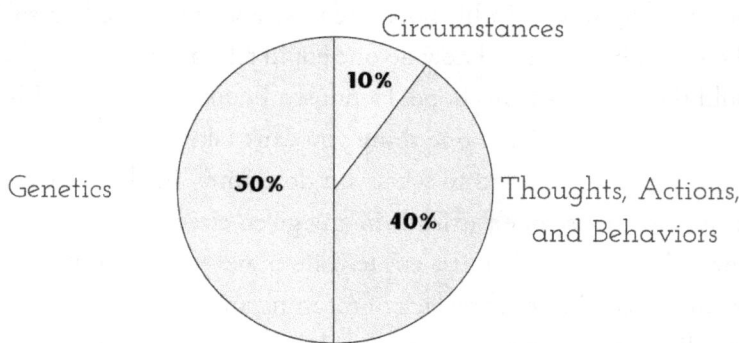

50 Percent Genetics

According to Lyubomirsky, 50 percent of our long-term happiness is based on genetics.[13] Basically, your sense of happiness comes from your biological mother or father or both. Yes, I know that some of you just dropped your heads and thought, "I'm so screwed." But stay with me.

Perhaps your happiness originates from the sunny, paternal side of your family. My dad is happy-go-lucky, doesn't get too worried or worked up about things, and tends to let most things just roll off his shoulder. He just goes with the flow and sees a lot of good in life. My momma is the most kind, nurturing person you would encounter, but her mind runs amok with worrisome thoughts much of the time. I can be prone to this anxiety as well.

Even if we reflect on our parents' moods, we may never know exactly what our genetic disposition is, but we do know that whatever fluctuations happen in our happiness, we tend to revert to this genetically determined set point for 50 percent of our happiness. We go up. We do down. But we always return to our baseline levels.

Don't be dissuaded yet. Perhaps our happiness set point cannot be changed, but this doesn't mean that we can't increase our happiness levels. Lyubomirsky's findings may be disappointing, but there is hope.

10 Percent External Circumstances

We may believe that if only our past and present circumstances could be changed, we could find a way to be happier. This conclusion may make it feel like happiness is totally out of our control. However, Lyubomirsky suggests that only about 10 percent of our long-term happiness comes from our external circumstances like our gender, age, ethnicity, where we grew up, and significant events that shaped our childhood, adolescence, and adulthood.[14]

In that light, negative events in childhood (such as parental divorce, a car accident, or bullying) and positive experiences (like family harmony, winning an award, or being popular) have only a small effect on our happiness. The same goes for significant events in our adult lives like our job, marital status, income, and living situation. But, as weighty as some of these events are, studies suggest that they account for only a small percentage of our happiness—just 10 percent!

It's especially easy to fall into the trap of thinking that happiness is purely an economic issue and that winning the lottery would solve all of our problems, but the research doesn't support that idea. While money can provide a range of benefits, such as better physical health, education, and safety, it is still one portion of that 10 percent of our happiness. So, while research says that income does correlate with happiness, the relationship is relatively weak. For example, surveys across nineteen nations reveal that the poor are only 20 percent less likely to report being satisfied with their lives than the rich. Especially once basic needs are met, money has a very small impact on happiness.[15]

We may place a tremendous emphasis on some life events as intimately tied to happiness. For example, we think of a wedding as the beginning of our "happy ending." This isn't true about becoming less happy for the rest of your life once you marry. You don't get less happy. You get a happiness boost for about two years and then you go back to baseline. Or for some people, you get unhappier.[16] Yes, it's at this point of my keynote when the crowd begins to belly laugh in their seats. In fact, a huge German study followed 1,761 people over fifteen years, starting when subjects were single and continuing until they became married and stayed married. Researchers found that on average, participants were no happier during the years after marriage than before and that the "marriage boost" in happiness lasted for only two years. After that, the subjects in the study returned to their set baseline happiness level, and some of their happiness levels got worse.[17]

Many parents feel that raising children is one of the most delightful and gratifying jobs, but it's also one of the most stressful and challenging responsibilities of our lives. Accordingly, research in positive psychology concludes that you become a little less happy when you become a parent.[18] Again, the crowd roars when I share this. Now, before some of you mommas come after me, let me just say that my son, Spencer, is hands down the biggest blessing in my life. He has brought immense joy and meaning to it. But being a parent is also hard, worrisome, and often scary.

Unsurprisingly, Lyubomirsky and colleagues explain that the link between happiness and parenting is complicated. "Parents are unhappy to the extent that they encounter relatively greater negative emotions, magnified financial problems, more sleep disturbance, and troubled marriages."[19] By contrast, when parents experience greater meaning in life, satisfaction in their basic needs, greater positive emotions, and enhanced social roles, they are met with happiness and joy. In other words, parenting leads us to heightened emotional experiences, for better and worse.[20] Parenting may be the most rewarding experience, but it is also the hardest and most humbling.

Let me give you a real-life example of how these external circumstances can rob us of our happiness—and trust me, I truly get why they do. Stephanie is a sixth-grade teacher who messaged me on Instagram two weeks before Christmas break. She wrote, "I'm drowning right now. School year 2021-2022 was focused on post-Covid trauma and behaviors. It drove focus away from instruction because of all the emotions and behaviors. Then 2022-2023 has been eaten up by more behaviors, IEP's, and closing the gap in achievement. Teachers are just trying to get by. My plate is so full. I have sixty students and less than ten are on a sixth-grade reading level. We test so much. I get it. They need rigor and challenging texts, but it's just so much. I teach sixth grade and I'm having to teach phonics. I didn't go to college to learn to teach phonics. I'm supposed to do all of this while also getting band-aids, sweeping the floor, and dealing with the discipline. Meanwhile, I'm also supposed to make my classroom door ready for Holiday Night all with a smile. It's overwhelming." I totally get why Stephanie let these external circumstances rob way more than 10 percent of her happiness. I have let and continue to let external circumstances steal bigger chunks of my happiness at times.

Our day-to-day lives revolve around the details of this 10 percent. It's easy to fall into the trap of thinking that satisfying our external wants or getting outside our present circumstances will fix everything. We think if we work harder, we will finally get enough money, enough status, or enough stuff to be happy. Or we feel that our problems are inhibiting a major portion of our happiness. But no matter what we do, the external circumstances in our lives will still only account for a small portion of what makes us happy.

There are times when we endure really hard experiences, and of course they're going to feel like they impact our happiness far more than 10 percent. But problems arise when those experiences impact our happiness for too long—when we stay in the gutter for too long. When we hold on to the injustices in our lives and we let them steal our joy, we may think we are holding on to them to uphold the righteousness we deserve, but at some point, we have to take responsibility for our lives. Only then can we step out of victim mode and into warrior mode.

40 Percent Thoughts, Actions, and Behaviors

We know that a large portion of our capacity for happiness depends on genetics and is therefore out of our control. We also know that while we can become happier by getting a raise, buying a new house, or losing weight, the boost in happiness is not long lasting. So, what can we do to increase our happiness long term?

Taking control of our own happiness comes down to the 40 percent of the pie chart that is left. That remaining portion is made up of three things: our thoughts, actions, and behaviors. This suggests that, by being intentional in our daily activities, we can increase our happiness levels.

The rest of this book focuses on ways that teachers can establish agency around happiness and emotional health by reframing our thoughts, actions, and behaviors with happiness habits. We can create a happier life—that power is within us. The ability to reprogram our brain, take different actions, and adopt different behaviors is within our reach.

Your thoughts become the beliefs you hold about yourself. A belief is just a repeating thought. Once you get more control over your thoughts, you begin to download new beliefs. When you're operating with a new belief system, this drives you to take different actions and form new habits. Once you have these new habits, you begin to experience a happier life.

Before we can be effective teachers, we have to take care of souls. Being a teacher is one of the most all-consuming professions you can go into, so sometimes it might seem like your entire identity is teaching, but your success in the classroom starts with work outside the classroom and inside yourself.

In the chapters that follow, we're going to focus mainly on the exciting 40 percent of the happiness pie that is within our control. We are going to talk about strategies that can make us happier people. We will explore strategies that will help lighten the heavy burden that teachers carry by focusing on what is within our control—by understanding that we have the power within us to live happy lives.

Chapter 3

KEEPING IT REAL

The Dark Side of Positivity Culture

My goal for this book is for you to walk away with a better understanding of what it takes to be happy, as well as some practical strategies for building emotional health. As you may have noticed by now, my approach to this project is to be authentic. After reading just a few chapters, you can see that I am willing to share myself—my struggles, failures, and imperfections. That is why I can't write about happiness without addressing a deterrent to true happiness, which is when a positive culture ignores reality and people's feelings. This chapter is here to keep it real.

We live in a world where people are obsessed with happiness. Stores are filled with signs that say "Life Is Good!" and "Choose Joy Every Day!" When we scroll through social media, we are bombarded with pictures of people's best moments. We're told to look for the silver lining when things feel tough in our jobs and our lives. Today, it feels like to succeed, we have to be happy . . . all the time. This means that when we're going through hard times, it can be difficult to talk about our big emotions. We're even told to "not go there." We are encouraged to look on the bright side or think positively, as if our heavy emotions are to be avoided like the plague. When we suppress our heavy emotions and don't talk about the hard things, it can lead to anxiety, depression, and burnout.

At the same time, it's not easy to be a teacher right now. We're supposed to please parents, answer to administrators, show support for our school, collaborate with our fellow teachers, and care for our students. We are expected to talk about the joy and magic of teaching, without showing signs of stress or weakness, even though the reality of teaching is hard. We're giving up our prep to cover a PE while the school finds a replacement, we're speaking with a concerned parent on the phone every day, or we're worrying about the young boy who dreads going home on Friday night because he doesn't know when he'll eat next. It is impossible to make it in this profession without some heavy feelings.

The underlying script is to not talk about these things because we need to stay focused on the positive. We're expected to play the role of the encouraging and optimistic teacher who keeps it all together and inspires students, but that's a load of BS. We are human and our jobs are stressful. If we don't start talking about the hard things in education, we can't get to the good stuff. When we lean in and acknowledge the vulnerabilities in this profession, we can move through them together to get to the other side.

We are allowed to feel the entire spectrum of emotions. We are allowed to feel hopelessness, anger, depression, sadness, disappointment, or frustration. We are allowed to have those feelings, and I don't believe that we talk about the hard feelings enough. While all of that is true, we also don't have to be owned by our emotions, and our emotions do not define us. The same is true for the thoughts we have; they are just thoughts, and they are not us. Emotions and thoughts are only a part of us at any given time.

As much as we should strive for happiness, it's important that we don't fall into the trap of toxic positivity. Instead, we need to learn how to embrace all of our emotions—both negative and positive—so that we can more fully inhabit our experiences. It's important, then, to distinguish between two forms of positivity: healthy and toxic.

Healthy positivity elicits feel-good emotions like joy, hope, gratitude, love, and happiness. Healthy positivity encompasses obviously healthy emotions like the ones listed above, but it also includes more subtle ones, such as curiosity, open-mindedness, generosity, harmony, and compassion. When we experience these emotions regularly, they can lead to transformations such as flourishing in our lives and being the best versions of ourselves. When we continually work to embody the best version of ourselves, we're able to tap into more of our potential, feel increased confidence, and experience more positive feelings. With healthy positivity, we are more likely to build positive habits in our lives that ultimately lead us to enjoy greater success, stronger relationships, and better health. Being happy doesn't mean we don't have bad days or feel sad sometimes; instead, it means we feel positive emotions more often than we do heavy ones. I don't like to call them negative emotions because there are no bad emotions. It's healthy to feel all our feelings, even the ones that feel heavy.

You might be asking yourself, "If all emotions are valid and important, then why does this project focus on working toward happiness?" The answer to this question is that we have to acknowledge and work through the hard stuff to get to the good stuff. We all want to feel happier and more at ease in our lives. When we can create happiness habits that increase our overall happiness levels, we experience more well-being, and then we're able to break out of some of the hardness of this job and create a better life for ourselves within this profession and outside of it.

As you'll learn in the next chapter, happiness is the very thing that leads to more success in our lives. Success can look like many things and is different for everyone. It might include the ability to enjoy your job more without letting it steal all the other parts of our lives, which can lead to resentment. It might be arriving home from school at a reasonable time so you have some extra hours to spend with your family. It could be deciding that your happiness makes you better at your job, better for your family, and most importantly better for yourself, which means you get to experience more feel-good emotions.

Toxic positivity is pretending everything is great when we're experiencing very real, heavy emotions. It's fake and feels riddled with guilt. It's the belief that no matter how difficult a situation is, we should focus on the good and maintain a positive mindset. Toxic positivity is disregarding any emotion that isn't optimistic. The reality is that life is not always sunshine and rainbows. We all go through hard situations and feel bad from time to time.

Many of you have likely experienced toxic positivity without even knowing it. Think of this example: You're behind on grading that's due on Friday, your dishwasher just broke, you're late for your son's soccer practice, and you have no idea what to cook for dinner. Then you tell someone how stressed you are and they say, "Now, sweetheart, just focus on all the good in your life. You're lucky to have that job and be able to take your child to their activity." That's toxic positivity!

Putting it bluntly, responses like this make me want to scream. Even if the person is right that we do have a good life, their response doesn't magically solve all the problems that are stressing us out at the moment. Instead, it makes us feel bad about our feelings, which doesn't help anything.

Toxic positivity may sound innocuous on the surface, but when we share something difficult with someone and they insist we turn it into something positive, what they're really saying is, as Dr. Susan David, author of *Emotional Agility*, says in a podcast interview with Brené Brown, "My comfort is more important than your reality."[21]

Toxic positivity is sometimes prevalent in our schools. We are told by well-intentioned leaders, "Every kid deserves your best!" or "Kids come first." Yet the people who are responsible for ensuring that students get the best—their teachers—are falling apart themselves. Yes, we want to be there for the kids, but that commitment to our students shouldn't come at the expense of our own well-being.

Sometimes "everything is fine," "things could be worse," or "stay positive" thinking takes precedence over truly troublesome behaviors and concerns, leaving us without substantive support. Laura, who is a member of our Teach Happy group on Facebook, describes the double bind of toxic positivity for educators:

> At times my class was absolutely overloaded. I had kids on every instructional level, above grade level, on grade level, and below grade levels. On top of that, I also had emotionally disordered kids, major behavior problems, learning problems, and so on. Because I worked to keep those kids out of the office and in my class, I continued to always get the challenging kids each year while other teachers didn't. I would discuss with the principal how difficult it was to meet the needs of these diverse students and that I needed some help, a break, or something because I was running on empty. He would always say, "Oh, I know you can handle it. You are so good! These kids need you." I always left feeling even worse than before I shared my struggle.

This leaves Laura feeling unseen and unheard, and it minimizes her human emotions. It's frustrating when our emotions aren't acknowledged, and it's toxic.

I've heard countless other stories like Laura's as I've worked with teachers across the country. One educator shared, "We're told over and over again that our school is here to support us and that we don't have to suffer in silence, but when we speak up, we are told we have a negative attitude regarding issues such as [being] short-staffed, no lunch break, and lack of support for our behaviorally challenged students."

While we don't want to be Cathy the Complainer all the time, and while having a positive outlook on our lives is helpful to our well-being, we still have many problems that need to be addressed, and we need to look for solutions. What if someone said to us, "I'm sorry you're having to absorb the overload of staffing issues, and it's not fair. This is a difficult situation and I'm glad you brought it up because it needs to be addressed." Wow, this would certainly make us feel better and help us shift to finding solutions.

We've all heard "We're a family," "It's about the outcome, not the income," "We do it for the students," "Teaching is a selfless profession," "If you just focus on building relationships," and "Be great for your students." All of these phrases are used to gaslight teachers by exuding a positive "feel" despite their toxic results. It's dismissing veiled issues and concerns by reminding teachers that we are expected to work overtime for free and handle stress with a smile.

It's easy to spot people in our lives who might be spreading toxic positivity, but most of the time we are both the perpetrator and the victim. It's possible that while reading this chapter you realized that you have participated in toxic positivity without even knowing it. I am guilty of this, too. That's okay! Often people have good intentions when spreading toxic positivity.

Inhabiting Our Emotions Fully

As teachers, we are told to be strong—in fact, we are praised for being strong and for moving on with our lives and growing through our challenges. An underlying narrative in education says that teachers need to be resilient and gritty, that if we have or feel difficult emotions there must be something wrong with us.

But we are allowed to experience all our emotions. We are allowed to feel anger, sadness, loneliness, and grief, as well as joy and happiness. These are normal human emotions. As Dr. David explains, "Emotions are these beautiful, yes, messy, yes, difficult, but beautiful signposts that allow us to understand ourselves better."[22]

I've talked a lot in this book about how hard it is to be a teacher right now. Ignoring the very real struggles of our occupation isn't helpful. I believe that we need to talk about the hard stuff within our schools and with our colleagues. We can acknowledge that we are overworked, underpaid, and downright exhausted. These are real feelings, and it is okay to acknowledge them. Ignoring hard feelings isn't helpful, and it can lead us to feel isolated. When we can talk about the hard stuff, we can move through heavy emotions and create forward momentum together.

I'm not promoting that we stay stuck in our heavy emotions, and much of this book is about actions and strategies we can try to get us out of the gutter quicker. But we are allowed to go in the gutter; we just don't stay there so long that we can't recapture the fullness of our lives. Instead, Dr. David suggests that we should start labeling our thoughts and emotions and the story they tell.[23] For example, teachers need to acknowledge how exhausted and frustrated they are from working long hours without extra compensation or appreciation. We cannot give ourselves compassion and start to work through these feelings until we identify them.

Personally, after I have identified my present emotion, it's important for me to decide how I can best allow myself to feel it. This might mean complaining or stepping away from people to be alone. Then, I extend some compassion toward myself. If I need to lie in bed for an afternoon and cry it out or eat my Hostess cupcakes, so be it. But the important thing is to allow yourself to identify the emotion, be curious about it, extend some compassion and kindness toward yourself, and eventually move through the emotion instead of getting stuck in it. Dr. Susan David calls this *emotional agility*, and she defines it as "the psychological skill that helps us to deal with the inner world of ours in a fundamentally healthy way."[24]

When you get stuck in emotions, you create a cycle of rumination that steals your happiness and well-being and increases your anxiety. When we brood, which we all do, this leads to feelings of hopelessness and victimhood. We want to move through this and eventually get to the other side. Simply naming our emotions can help us to experience them more fully and also more productively.

Research shows that expressing and processing your emotions can help you to weather even the most difficult situations. For example, a study conducted by a team at the University of Iowa showed that during the pandemic, people who acknowledged and checked in with their emotions experienced less stress than those who tried to shove their feelings down.[25] Taking note of our emotions allows us to honor what is happening in our lives and think about what we can actually do to help the problem.

Building Healthy Positivity

Working toward healthy positivity, and dismantling toxic positivity, can be as easy as a three-step process. When a friend or colleague comes to you with a difficult situation, do your best to:

1. Listen
This sounds obvious, but often when people are upset or stressed out, they just want to be heard. Putting down your phone and actively listening is a great way to tell someone that you are there for them.

2. Acknowledge Feelings
Simply acknowledging someone's problems and emotions tells them that you've heard them and that their feelings are valid.

3. Offer Help
Even if you think you have the perfect solution, hold off on offering unsolicited advice. Instead, ask what you can do to help. This lets the other person know that you are there to support them.

We can use these same three steps when we notice our inner critic creeping out too. If you are slow and sluggish one day, take a minute and try to listen to what your body is telling you instead of chugging a coffee and telling yourself to snap out of it.

When you're feeling down about teaching, take time to acknowledge how you're feeling. Maybe you're stuck in a rut at work, and it's been making you unmotivated. Accept that those are your feelings. Then, think about how you can support yourself. It could be that you need to get out the door by 4:00, attend a professional development workshop that invigorates your teaching practice, or simply give yourself some grace along the way.

These steps don't just apply to teachers either. All of us are probably guilty of telling our students that everything is fine and to shake it off. Young children are still learning how to process their emotions, and when adults tell them that everything is fine, even when they're experiencing heavy emotions, it tells children not to listen to their feelings. When a child is crying because they spilled water on their favorite drawing, it's easy for us to tell them, "It's not a big deal, just draw another one!" But even that is toxic positivity. The problem might seem trivial to us, but the emotions the child is having are very real.

Failing to validate a student's emotions also might make them less likely to share their feelings with you in the future. Think back to the very first chapter of this book, where I talked about my former student Corey. Sometimes all students need to be successful is to have someone listen to their problems and really care about what they're going through. Not only is empathy going to make them better students, and impact your classroom positively, but it's also going to help your students gain confidence so they can grow into well-adjusted adults.

Chapter 4

REDEFINING HAPPINESS

A New Formula for Teacher Success

We have been taught a clear formula for success. According to that old formula, we need to go to school, work hard, and get good grades in order to graduate at the top of the class. That academic success then leads to a top-notch college where competition continues, so it's time to get even more serious. If we work hard, we can land a good internship, which will lead to a good job. If we continue to work hard at the job for many years, we will make more money so that we can buy a nice car, live in a big home, get married, and have 2.5 kids. And then, once we have done all of these things, we can consider ourselves successful—and then we will finally be happy.

Putting it simply, we are programmed to believe that first we find success and then we can be happy. I want to let you all in on a little secret though: happiness actually drives our success, not the other way around. More than this, we have the power to determine our own happiness with specific strategies. According to Shawn Achor's remarkable research, "What we're finding is that it's not necessarily reality which shapes us, it's the lens through which your brain views the world that shapes your reality . . . If we can change the lens, not only can we change your happiness we can change every single educational and business outcome at the same time."[26]

If we are going to transform our relationship to happiness, we need to confront our cultural scripts regarding happiness. We cannot afford to continue to think of happiness as a reward that is forever in the future. By dispelling our cultural myths around happiness, we can reframe our understanding of emotional health and reclaim our agency, cultivating happiness *in the present.*

The If/When Game

Our ideas around happiness don't just place it in the future; they also suggest that happiness is utterly conditional. In that vein, we often play an if/when game with our happiness. For example, we continually tell ourselves that "I'll be happy when I lose thirty pounds" or "I'll be happy if . . . I have a more attentive spouse." As educators, we might say, "I'll be happy when I have a better class" or even "I'll be happy if I get a better job."

There are many potential problems with this thinking. We learned in chapter 2 that external circumstances only account for about 10 percent of our happiness levels. So, I may believe that if I can buy a condo in Florida, I'll be substantially happier. A divorcée might undergo cosmetic surgery to make her feel younger and more attractive, believing that she'll feel happier. Or a thirty-year-old might land the job of his dreams and think it will make him happier. But all of us will only be temporarily happy from the achievement of these things. After some time, we will return to our baseline, and the happiness bubble will burst.

This same thing happens each time we meet a goal as part of the process that Achor calls the hedonic treadmill, "the idea that we get accustomed to any success we experience and simply set new goals."[27]

So, when Achor worked at Harvard, he observed that it didn't take students very long before they got over the excitement of being accepted to an Ivy League school; they quickly fell into routines of worry over classes and the stress of their workload.[28]

Achor explains the hedonic treadmill more fully in his highly popular TED talk, "The Happiness Advantage." He argues, "Every time your brain achieves success, you change the goalpost of what success looks like. You got good grades, now you have to get better grades. You got a good job, now you have to get a better job. You hit your sales target, now I'm going to change your sales target."[29]

For teachers, this means striving to add more and more to your plate. I'm sure we all know a teacher at our school who is praised for being a "superstar!" At times, administrators praise teachers who tutor students after school, who take on the challenging students, and who volunteer to help with the Christmas fair, all while being amazing teachers. This praise and validation can cause them to look for more ways to volunteer so they can receive more praise. This is the hedonic treadmill and it's unsustainable. Those teachers will continue to strive for more and more responsibility until eventually they get burned out and are forced to step away.

The success-first model is also related to the if/when game we play with our happiness. It's the idea that we can't be happy until we are successful. Many times, we hear teachers say "I'll be happy when I retire" or "I'll be happy when I get a better class next year." Again, I want to acknowledge that this profession can be extremely difficult. Heck, I recently read that teachers make approximately 1,500 decisions per day.[30] No wonder you're playing the if/when game. "I'll be happy when I don't have to respond to all the emails, deal with the overly involved parent, and answer 250 questions in the span of an hour."

But why do we have to be successful before we allow ourselves to be happy? The answer is we don't! We know from learning about the hedonic treadmill that it is very difficult to actually see ourselves as successful because our definition of success changes. When we play the if/when game with happiness, we are constantly putting off our happiness. We are tying our happiness to the achievement of a goal, which means we aren't allowed to feel happiness until we've reached it. I'm all about goals, and I believe that you should have goals and a vision for your life. Goals are great. When we have a vision for our life and we are working toward it, we feel more satisfied and fulfilled in life. But when we link happiness to the attainment of that vision or those goals, we are missing out on happiness right now! We are allowed to be happy in the now. Happiness is not a conditional feeling.

The New Formula

We must reverse the happiness blueprint we learned and develop a new, healthier model. It should be based on strong research that concludes happiness is the very thing that leads to success. There's nothing wrong with achievements and aspiring to do and be more in life. There's nothing wrong with living in a big home or having money. But when we depend on those things to bring us happiness, we will be left feeling empty.

If the success-first recipe for happiness worked, every person we know who's skinny, fit, beautiful, or rich would be blissfully happy, and obviously, that is not the case. This is why social and emotional learning needs to find its way into our classrooms and workplaces. Teaching skills related to social-emotional well-being are not an extra—these skills are at the heart of what our students need to find happiness and success. (Notice I said happiness first!)

Happiness also drives success at a systemic level. I work with school leaders, CEOs, bosses, and managers who are a bit iffy about this whole "happiness in the workspace" idea, but they're starting to see the light. Instead of focusing on hard work, putting in more hours, and increasing test scores, sales output, or revenue (which all lead to burnout), they are learning that happiness truly helps their employees be more engaged, productive, and inspired. In contrast, when an employee is unhappy, overworked, and feels unseen, they usually also lack optimism; they are less productive, less efficient, and more stressed.

Beyond the personal benefits, happiness yields big-time dividends. Achor's research shows that a brain in a positive state is 31 percent more productive than a brain that is negative, neutral, or stressed.[31] Let's pretend a principal has an app on her phone, and throughout the day she can tap on the app to get a reading on every employee in the building. How many teachers do you think would be operating in a positive state?

Happiness also drives performance. Studies have found that doctors are 19 percent faster and more accurate at coming up with the correct diagnosis when they are in a positive state versus a negative or neutral one. Employees are three times more creative and ten times more engaged in their job when they are in a positive state. When we can find a way to be positive, we're able to work harder, faster, and more intelligently.[32] Helping employees live happier lives is not just better for them; it's better for the schools and businesses they work for too!

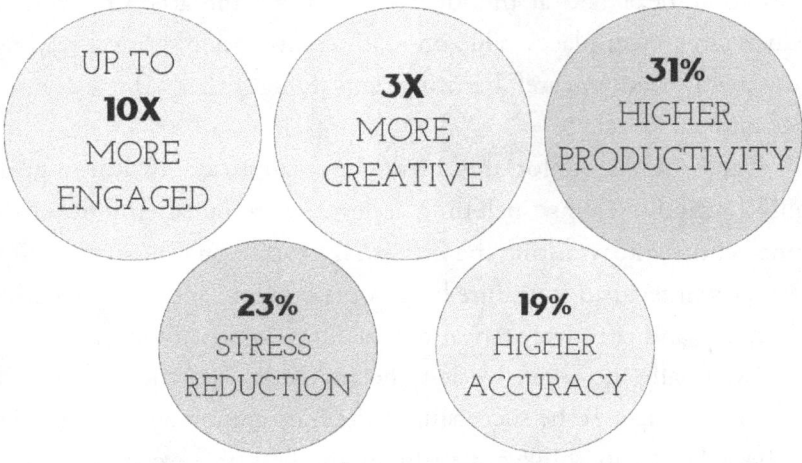

HAPPINESS FUELS SUCCESS

UP TO 10X MORE ENGAGED

3X MORE CREATIVE

31% HIGHER PRODUCTIVITY

23% STRESS REDUCTION

19% HIGHER ACCURACY

Research from Shawn Achor

Positive psychology researchers have also done a meta-analysis, which is a study of almost every scientific happiness study available, and guess what? Their discoveries matched Shawn Achor's studies. Achor states, "Happiness leads to success in nearly every domain, including work, health, friendship, sociability, creatively, and energy."[33]

Teaching Happiness

This new perspective on the relationship between happiness and success begs us, as educators, to consider how schools are playing into this outdated formula for success. Our school system actively contributes to our distorted understanding of success as a reward for hard work, but as teachers we are uniquely situated to intervene by offering our students—and ourselves—strategies for fostering happiness habits that will drive success.

Most of us would agree that 90 percent of the school day is focused on left-brained intelligence. Almost all education systems have a hierarchy of subjects. Mathematics and language arts are at the top, humanities come next, and at the lonely bottom are the arts. Our current education system places value on math computation, critical reading, rote memorization, careful writing, and thought that is logical, rational, and analytical.

There's a reason for this hierarchical approach to learning: all public school systems, including colleges, were invented around the nineteenth century during the Industrial Revolution. During this time factory workers had to endure long hours of work, and they needed to efficiently and effectively repeat the same task over and over again.

Eventually, however, we left the industrial age and entered the information age. To be successful in the information age, you needed to be a left-brain thinker. Left-brain thinkers are excellent readers, memorizers, regurgitators of knowledge. They excel in mathematics, computation, and the core academic skills. This era favored people who excelled academically and generated the creation of our modern school system.

Now we have left the information age and entered the conceptual age. This age is more focused on right-brain thinking such as creativity, big-picture thinking, empathy, meaning, and purpose. We are discovering and yearning for a life that feels really good to us and isn't just about functionality but about feeling, enjoying, and being fully alive. We live in a time when creating and empathizing are the skills needed for success. What we need now is creativity, the arts, play, meaning, mission, and relationships. To thrive, we need emotional intelligence over academic intelligence. Dan Pink, author of *A Whole New Mind*, states, "Key abilities will not be high tech but high touch, and we will value the ability to make meaning and connections in a world where information is a commodity."[34] Basically, the information age is no longer needed because information is at our fingertips. According to Dan Pink, we are entering a whole new age that focuses on a different set of skills.

But how much time do we spend teaching students how to mediate stress, handle conflict, develop healthy relationships, foster strong communication skills, and navigate life and the world around them? State curriculum standards and school policies dictate what to teach our students. This means we don't have time to teach the skills that our students need to be set up for success. We are working in an outdated school system that is still driven by traditional grades and standardized tests.

Although we've entered a new age, most school systems have remained the same, and our students' needs for success are not being served. Even if we *did* have the time to teach emotional intelligence, many of us are still working on cultivating those skills ourselves. We weren't taught how to embrace failure, resolve conflict, maintain strong relationships, have self-awareness, or navigate emotions and feelings when we were in school; as a result, we won't be able to teach those skills until we have adequate resources for doing so.

Sadly, teachers are leaving the profession because of how demanding the job has become, but what might be possible if schools embraced these insights and started using a happiness-first model? If teachers were happy in their lives, they would be more willing to stay in their career. They'd work more efficiently and with less stress. This transformation would impact not just teachers but also the next generation of children.

To lead that sea change in education, a couple of years ago I created the Teach Happy Academy, through which I have supported over seventeen schools and districts, as well as thousands of teachers. Yes, I love doing keynotes and getting educators fired up, but everyone goes back to the abyss of their desks and classrooms, and it's easy to toss everything I taught them out the door. With the Teach Happy Academy, I created a nine-month social-emotional wellness course and group coaching program that walks educators through the school year. The program yields results by giving teachers a step-by-step, proven framework that helps them learn to manage stress, create more flow in their lives, and make happiness part of their everyday experience. As you've seen, studies show that when we learn to place our happiness first, we see increases in performance, productivity, and engagement.

Want to learn more about the Teach Happy Academy? Use this QR code to get started.

When we put happiness first, we change every other area in our lives. We are better at our jobs, and we feel better as parents, friends, and partners. Happiness first means that we are no longer working toward a goal that won't actually solve our problems. Instead, we are enjoying the journey of life and celebrating our accomplishments along the way.

Chapter 5

THE ART OF FLOW

Forget Everything You Know about Work-Life Balance

Even though teachers come to school every day and put on a smile for their students, a report by Education Support revealed that nearly 75 percent of teachers and 84 percent of school leaders admit they are stressed at their jobs. This is hardly surprising when almost one-third of teachers work more than sixty hours a week and 82 percent of teachers said their workload is unmanageable.[35]

Despite these statistics, teachers' workloads have only gotten heavier. Two-thirds reported that expectations had increased significantly over the last five years and that their workload was affecting their physical and mental health. It's no surprise then that only 12 percent of teachers say that they have a good work-life balance.[36]

Like most of you, I felt the immense stress of being a teacher and school leader. It felt like there was always something new being added to my plate. Now I'm supposed to be trauma-informed and create a safe environment for students. Now I'm going to need to relearn how to teach reading because there's a more scientific way of doing so. Now we are going to implement this initiative, which requires additional paperwork, meetings, trainings, and time at home to figure it out.

I want to reiterate that I know the teaching profession is tough, and I know it feels almost impossible to think that you can free up any space to make real change happen. I hold out hope that someday the education system will change for teachers, but it's not something we can count on. It might always be a system where teachers are held to impossible standards and are never paid what they are worth. Since we can't snap our fingers and change the system, we have to focus on the one thing we do have control over: ourselves.

The expectations placed on teachers over the last decade have become unrealistic. These statistics are startling but likely not a big surprise to educators. Work cultures in education do not adequately support educators' happiness, and educators' stress levels negatively impact education in turn. However, if teachers can reframe their approach to work-life balance, then they—and their students—can reap the benefits of emotional health. As a critical concept, flow can help us to move toward work-life balance.

Understanding Stress

The effects of stress on the human brain are disastrous. When the human brain is stressed, it cannot function at its full capacity. As teachers, we see this phenomenon in our students. Students who are experiencing stress have tantrums, throw desks, flee, or exhibit other behavior problems because their brain is shutting down. This same principle is true for stressed adults.

Brain research has helped us to understand why the effects of stress are so catastrophic. When stressed, our prefrontal cortex, which governs our highest cognitive abilities, becomes impaired. This means that our executive functioning, decision-making, and focused-attention functioning decrease, even as our anxiety levels increase.

When our prefrontal cortex is under stress, the amygdala—the part of the brain that regulates our emotional activity—takes over, which causes mental paralysis and panic. Our decision-making is inhibited, and our emotions override our cognitive abilities. We can't think straight, and we make decisions based on emotional reactivity rather than logical thinking.

At the same time, when we are stressed, cortisol streams through our bodies. Cortisol is the primary stress hormone, and heightened cortisol increases sugars (glucose) in our bloodstream, which sends us into fight-or-flight mode. Thankfully, most adults under stress can control their emotions and resist throwing things or stomping on the ground, but they still aren't able to think clearly.

When we consider what is happening in the brain and body when we're stressed, it's no wonder that teachers are struggling. It's easy to understand why teachers are emotionally frayed, spent, and running around without direction. The question is, how can we bring balance into our lives?

Working with Flow

Well, to be honest, I despise the word *balance*, so I'm going to propose another word and a different way to think about balance. I think of balance as trying to hold all the important aspects of my life in my arms. When one of the elements of my life gets particularly busy—for example, when I have to travel for work—I end up dropping something else, like my marriage. Then I'll try to pick that up and set aside time to be with my husband, but next I'll feel like I've dropped nurturing my hobbies. Balance feels like an unattainable goal we're all supposed to be striving for, trying to find the middle ground between our family, parenting, marriage, work, life, etc. I think it's an unrealistic expectation, and it leaves us guilt-ridden—which sometimes actually causes more stress.

Balance just does not work for me. I suggest that we bring another word into our vocabulary to describe the need to be at peace with all the competing elements in our lives: *flow*.

I know that flow has several different meanings, and the way I'm using it here is different from any of them. In positive psychology, for example, flow means that sweet spot of activity where we are so totally engaged with what we're doing that we're at ease and full of energy.[37] The flow that I'm talking about is not the same, although it certainly has some similar characteristics.

I imagine flow as being on a raft that's floating down a stream. For a while, when things are calm, I might focus my energy on my spiritual health, but if the current picks up, I might need to redirect by looking into my finances. This doesn't mean I'm dropping my spiritual health; it just means I'm going with the flow of my life and giving my attention to the areas that need it.

Flow is now what I work toward in my life. The notion of flow puts me at ease and feels softer and more aligned with how I want to live. Flow feels like everything is moving in the right direction. It's energy that is creative, productive, and has forward momentum. Feeling flow means that I feel really good a lot of the time in the important aspects of my life. I feel good a lot of the time in my parenting, but not perfect. I feel good in my marriage a lot of the time, but there are still things I could work on. I feel good about my career a lot of the time, but yes, I still get stressed.

Flow means we quit fighting so hard. We stop the mentality that tells us to grind, struggle, and push through. Instead, we embrace being more in sync with the areas of our lives that are important. When I'm in flow in the important areas of my life, I feel energized, creative, and fulfilled. In flow, we don't see the important areas of our lives competing but rather working in unison. Of course, we still must make choices, but the choices don't pit things that are all important to us against each other.

When it comes to education, flow can be a complete game changer. Teachers already have to juggle different tasks in the classroom. They switch from supervising students to curriculum meetings with other teachers, then to calls with parents, then back to teaching students. These very different tasks are almost impossible to balance, but when we reframe our thinking, it becomes manageable. When teachers start to think about their lives in terms of flow, they will realize that it's okay to let some things go while giving their full attention to others. Yes, it means we must embrace perfection so we can enjoy the other parts of our lives.

While the flow mindset is helpful for classroom tasks, it's even more important to implement in life outside the classroom. For example, if it's the week before standardized testing, you might have to skip book club to prepare extra material for students. But if your child is having a tough time at school, then you might devote your evenings to spending time with them even if it means getting behind on grading. Flow is all about setting your priorities and not feeling guilty about them.

Building toward Flow

When we're used to thinking of life in terms of balance, it can be difficult to embrace flow as an alternative. The Wheel of Life is a tool that I use to help people zero in on areas of their life they want to focus on. The original idea behind the Wheel of Life came from industry pioneer Paul J. Meyer in the 1960s, and it's a way to help people actualize their goals. The wheel is a circle with spokes, resembling a bicycle wheel. It's used to present the most important aspects of life, which are identified as the next image shows.[38]

How Can We Use the Wheel of Life?

The Wheel of Life provides a snapshot of our well-being and our level of life satisfaction. By scoring each category, we identify areas that need

THE WHEEL OF LIFE

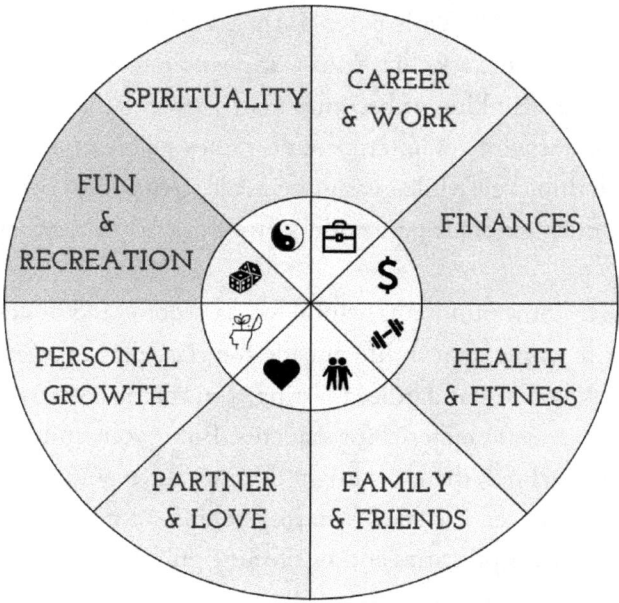

support and improvement so that we can reach individual and overall life goals. But most importantly, it helps us see how we want to feel.

We can use our scores to look at where we feel we are in flow and where we might need to focus our attention a little more. It's a great tool to help us figure out what areas are meeting our needs and making us feel good and which ones leave us feeling dissatisfied and unfulfilled.

These are the categories I recommend most people examine, but everyone who uses the Wheel of Life should customize it to meet their needs and personal priorities. As you examine the Wheel of Life and answer the questions below for each category, remember that this is just a way to start thinking about what areas of your life are in flow and which could use improvement. You're not going to be able to answer yes to all these questions, and that's okay! They are intended as a tool for reflection rather than a checklist.

Categories

1. **Career & Work:** In the work category, we can think about the job we are currently working and how satisfied we are with it.
Questions to ask yourself:

    - Am I happy where I'm at as an educator, or would I rather be in a different school or different position?
    - Does my career path currently bring me happiness?
    - Does my teaching job leave me feeling drained?
    - Am I motivated to advance in my career?
    - Am I excited to go to work most days?

2. **Finances:** This category refers to our success in managing, budgeting, saving, and investing money.
Questions to ask yourself:

    - Do I have enough money to do things that bring me joy?
    - Do I stress about finances?
    - Do I have bills and debt I am not able to pay?
    - Do I have an emergency fund?
    - Do finances affect my self-esteem?

3. **Health & Fitness:** This category can be used to represent our physical, mental, and emotional health.
Questions to ask yourself:

    - How do I feel?
    - Do I regularly exercise or move my body in some way?
    - What are my eating habits?
    - Do I get adequate sleep?
    - Are there any changes I'd like to make to live a healthier lifestyle?

4. **Family & Friends:** This category asks us to evaluate our relationships with other people. Happiness research says building social

connections is one of the top five happiness habits, so this aspect of our lives is especially important to nourish.

Questions to ask yourself:

- Do my relationships feel good?
- Do any of them need work?
- Are they satisfying to me?
- Are they having a positive influence on my life?
- Am I giving adequate time to social circles?

5. **Partner/Love:** This category asks us to examine our current partnership or marriage since it is one of the most important relationships we have.

   Questions to ask yourself:

   - Are my partner and I making time for each other?
   - Are we supporting and listening to each other?
   - Do we have fun together?
   - Do our values and long-term goals align?

6. **Personal Growth:** This category represents the time we spend working toward personal goals.

   Questions to ask yourself:

   - Am I learning, growing, and developing as a person?
   - Am I working on myself and taking responsibility for my life?
   - Do I have goals I am actively working toward?
   - Do I feel challenged?
   - Am I seeking out resources that interest me and help me grow?

7. **Fun and Recreation:** This category refers to what we do in our free time away from work or other obligations.

   Questions to ask yourself:

   - What kinds of activities do I engage in to bring myself life satisfaction, such as sports, reading, writing, or any other hobby?

- How much time am I able to devote to play or hobbies?
- Do I seek out new hobbies or interests?
- How do I engage in a fun way with life?
- What do I do to play?

8. **Spirituality:** This category asks us to consider our inner world. It focuses on our inner peace, a sense of connection with the divine, and how we connect with ourselves.
Questions to ask yourself:

- Do I feel a connection between my mind, body, and spirit?
- Do I have spiritual practices, like going to church or meditating?
- Do I feel like something is missing in my life spiritually?
- What is my definition of higher powers?
- What do I do to help myself feel at peace?

Remember, these categories can be changed to fit individual needs. Here are a couple of other examples that could work for you.

9. **Physical Environment:** For some people, immediate surroundings are an important element in creating flow in their life.
Questions to ask yourself:

- How do I feel in my home?
- Does having unorganized spaces around make my mind feel cluttered?
- How do my car, home, desk, and clothes reflect my inner world?
- What about my physical environment brings me joy and satisfaction?
- Where do I feel the most comfortable?

10. **Contribution:** This category may overlap with relationships, work, or recreation, but it has unique characteristics that are important for some people.

Questions to ask yourself:

- In what ways do I help others?
- Do I volunteer my time or resources?
- To what extent am I active in the community?
- Are there causes I am passionate about?
- How do I feel I can make the world a better place?

After answering these questions, you might notice that certain categories were particularly hard to assess, and that's okay! No one has their life perfectly together, but with the proper tools and focus, we can begin to improve the areas in our lives that are most important to us. Believe me, as I reread these questions, I had a moment of inferiority until I reminded myself that the questions are not a checklist; they are just a starting point for reflection.

Rank the Categories

Once we've answered all these questions, it should be easy to tell which areas in our lives are important and where we'd like to redirect our energy and attention to implement flow. The next step to a healthy life flow is to rank the categories and reflect on them.

1. Think about how satisfied you are with each aspect of your life. Rank each category on a scale from 1 to 10, with 10 being ideal and 1 meaning that there is a lot of room for improvement. Don't overthink it; just go with your gut.
2. Now, look at your scores. What are the top three areas of your life that, if you worked on improving them in this next year, would make the biggest difference when it comes to flow and feeling good? The key is to use the Wheel of Life to think about how we can bring more flow into our lives. We don't necessarily want to focus on the areas that we ranked the lowest.

Once you've assessed and ranked each category, decide on focus areas for the next year. Then take some time to reflect on the following questions:

1. Looking at your first priority, consider what you want to improve. Why is this important? How will it improve your life?
2. If you don't work on this area, what are the consequences? How will this impact you and your life over the next year?
3. What would it look like to be living your ideal life in this category? *Feel* what it is like and *visualize* your ideal day, week, month, or year. The more detail, the better!
4. What could you do today to move your current score up one point to your ideal score?
5. Decide on an achievable action to bring yourself one step closer to your target.

It's easy for us to get overwhelmed and feel like we're failing in all of these areas, but remember we just have to move the needle a little bit; we don't have to fix every aspect of our lives at once. I recommend focusing on those three top areas first. Why? When we are hyper-focused and concentrate on three areas of life, we can implement change and improve. Then, once we start to see those aspects of our lives improve, it creates a domino effect and everything else begins to improve too.

Once we start feeling better in one area, we can begin to navigate another area. For instance, if we start feeling better in our career, we can begin to navigate parenting with a bit more ease. If we feel like we have stabilized our bank account, then our physical environment may start to improve. If we spend time enjoying family and friends, it is likely to bleed into our hobbies and fun. For example, I discovered that I wasn't doing a good job in the fun and recreation category or the friend category. I was too tired on Friday evening to head out to dinner with friends and just wanted to sit on my couch and binge-watch

Outlander. I decided to focus on the fun and recreation category. What was something I'd been wanting to do that sounded fun? Pickleball! I'd been hearing about this sport, but hadn't acted on it. I texted four of our friend couples and asked if anyone wanted to learn with me. A year later and we now play a couple of times a week, so I'm upping the score in both categories now, fun and recreation, and friends! Focusing on one category ended up affecting another, and it's really contributed to my well-being.

The process of writing down, reviewing, and rating areas not only provides input for the goal-setting process, but it also offers insights into aspects of our lives that are causing us difficulty. From there, the work moves toward creating more flow in life and the ripple effect begins.

Working on flow can bring us satisfaction and peace as we continually reflect on the many important areas in our lives. Flow allows us to feel satisfied in most areas without triggering dissatisfaction when we can't achieve perfection. We deserve to feel at peace. We can't beat ourselves up, trying to find balance by putting all the important areas of our lives in competition with one another. Reclaiming our happiness means hopping into the lazy river to feel at ease and find flow in our lives.

Chapter 6

WORDS HAVE POWER

Using Gratitude to Rewire Your Brain for Happiness

For the last ten years, my daily practice of gratitude has probably been one of the most impactful practices in my life. My relationship with my husband is stronger. My sense of connection to my spirit is deeper. It helps me to see more good than bad, and it shifts my thinking toward abundance and goodness more often than not.

I know we've all heard of practicing gratitude before, and trust me, Oprah preached the value of gratitude to me for years and I still didn't incorporate it into my daily routine. Honestly, I didn't believe that saying three things I'm grateful for each day would make me happier. As always, though, my dear mentor, Oprah, knew what she was talking about.

When we practice gratitude, our brains begin to scan for more goodness in our lives. This doesn't mean we are blind to the hard stuff or the messy parts of our lives. But because it allows us to see even the tiniest glimpses of goodness, gratitude helps us navigate our heavier feelings or burdens.

Practicing gratitude is a concrete action that can improve our lives, and its effectiveness is also backed by scientific research. When we start to think more positively, our brain chemistry changes. These optimistic and grateful thoughts release what I like to call happy chemicals: dopamine, serotonin, and oxytocin. They make us feel even happier.

People who practice gratitude aren't just happier; they also report having fewer aches and pains, exercising more, and experiencing reduced symptoms of depression. Practicing gratitude also improves sleep and increases self-esteem.[39]

One of the reasons why I believe gratitude is such an important tool for teachers is because teaching is tough, and it's easy to hyper-focus on the hundred hard things we deal with daily. But that little one- or two-minute habit of thinking about what went well each day can shift your brain back to positive, and this can give you a more optimistic view of the work you're doing on behalf of students.

Once teachers have begun to master this habit, I encourage them to begin modeling it for their students. I began class each day with ninety seconds of gratitude. We would go around the room and everyone would state one thing they were thankful for. This quickly gave students the opportunity to hear everyone's gratitude. Then, at the end of the day, my students would whip out their spiral notebooks (gratitude journals) and write down three things they were thankful for that day. My goal was for students to leave my classroom each day not just as better readers, writers, and mathematicians, but also as people who would be better at life.

The average human being has about seventy thousand thoughts a day.[40] Seventy thousand thoughts! And we also know that for the average human being, about 80 percent of those thoughts are negative.[41] This means that when the average person puts their head on the pillow at night, they have had fifty-six thousand negative thoughts!

You might be thinking, "Jeez, why are humans so negative?" Again, scientific research helps us answer this question. The amygdala is the part of our brain responsible for keeping us safe. It is thanks to our amygdala that 80 percent of thoughts in a day are negative and that 95 percent of those are the same thoughts we had the day before.[42] Crazy, right?

Sometimes referred to as the lizard brain (because it's the oldest part of our brain), the amygdala helped our ancestors survive millions of years ago. When early humans spotted a saber-toothed tiger nearby, the amygdala would activate the sympathetic nervous system and trigger an acute stress response that would prepare the body to fight, flee, or freeze. If our ancestors escaped, the amygdala would store the details of the dangerous situation they faced to prevent it from happening again. The sound of a growl would trigger a memory of danger and allow early humans to react even more quickly in threatening situations. The more stressful the experience, the stronger the memory.

Since then, our brain has barely evolved, but our environment has completely changed. Now, humans don't have to worry about a saber-toothed tiger attacking them on the way to the mailbox. The problems humans have today are much more abstract, and most of the time not life-threatening, but our amygdala is still searching for danger. This means that instead of keeping us safe, the amygdala is just keeping us stressed.

A team of researchers performed a study on the amygdala by placing participants in an MRI machine and showing them positive, neutral, and negative images. Participants' amygdalae were activated as soon as they were shown a negative picture, but they did not activate when participants saw a positive image until the researcher asked them to focus on what was in the picture. This shows that our brain has learned to have quicker and stronger reactions to negative stimuli.[43]

Our neurological bias toward perceiving negativity has also been transformed by modern society. Because of advancements in technology, we are not only seeing our own experiences, but we are also surrounded by negativity. We scroll through our phones and see people complaining on social media. When we turn on the news, we are faced with headlines about people suffering all over the world. All this negativity makes our amygdala go crazy!

Why Gratitude Works

Now, I know all of this is discouraging, but there is hope! While we may be predisposed to focus on the negative, research also shows that if we write down three things we are thankful for every day for twenty-one days, we can rewire our brain. This short and simple gratitude practice creates a new neural feedback loop.[44]

So, what are neuro feedback loops? Well, I want you to imagine that we have all of these roads in our brain—hundreds and hundreds of roads. Whatever road we travel the most is the one with the deepest grooves, which means it's the one we return to more easily.

For example, some of us have feedback loops that constantly tell us how frustrated we are with our job. When something bad happens at work, that experience supports our opinion that our job is frustrating, so we continue to look for and expect bad things to happen at work. The more we travel down that road, the deeper those ruts in our thinking become. After a while, the idea that our job is frustrating becomes our default route. This happened to me with another teacher. There was a teacher in my school who drove me crazy. In my opinion, he was lazy, rude, and only there to collect his paycheck and retire in ten more years. The more I focused on his faults, the more faults I could find. Now it's not just that he's lazy, but he's also walking down the hall like a curmudgeon. I don't like the way he fake smiles at me. I don't like how he walks or how he balks at any and everything that's asked of him. I quickly noticed that the more I focused on this teacher, it was like the more evidence I was getting of all of his faults. So I forced myself to notice one good thing about him each time I saw him because I didn't like how much energy he was taking from me. While I still don't admire this man, I noticed that I was able to shift my focus a bit with him and eventually saw a few good things he was contributing. Bottom line is that he still wasn't there for the right reasons, but I learned to shift a bit toward gratitude and compassion and away from all the negative thinking patterns about him that kept growing.

Over time, though, gratitude allows us to establish new cognitive routes that lead us to happier emotional destinations. I've had a daily gratitude practice for over ten years, and it has changed my life. Getting started with a gratitude practice can be difficult, but it helps to establish consistent habits. My gratitude journal stays on a wooden tray on my dining room table because each morning, I know I'm going to have my protein shake at that table. I always start by putting the date in the corner, and then I write the words "I am thankful . . ." along the top of the page.

I always start with this prompt to capitalize on the insights of the great Dr. Wayne Dyer, who was an internationally known author in the field of personal development. He teaches that *I AM* are two of the most powerful words you can use to begin a sentence, and the important thing is what words you use to finish that sentence. Anytime you start a sentence with I am, you are creating what you are and what you want to be. He wrote, "The words I am, which you consistently use to define who you are and what you are capable."[45]

With my prompt on the page, I begin to reflect on things for which I'm thankful. Research shows we must write down three different things, but I choose to write down five. Your gratitude also needs to be specific. "I am thankful for my family" is too general. Try something like this instead: "I am thankful my mom listened to me today while I cried about Spencer moving to Boston." (True story.) If we are thankful for our health, we might write "I'm thankful that my body allows me to freely move about my day and get things done."

> I am thankful... 3/23/23
>
> 1. Thursday night pizza with Scott, Mom, & Dad.
> 2. Spencer got the job in Boston!
> 3. The daily hugs and snuggles I get from our dogs, George, Sophie, and Luna.
> 4. My body that allows me to run 40 miles per week.
> 5. The daffodils sitting on my office desk.

When I taught, I also practiced gratitude in my classroom, which I shared in the chapter about Corey. Given how transforming that practice was for Corey, for my other students, and for my life as a teacher, I now encourage teachers to start the day with ninety seconds of gratitude. As part of that practice, I invite teachers to go around the room asking every student to state one thing they are grateful for. You can do this at a fast pace, and by the end, every student will have been exposed to maybe twenty-seven expressions of gratitude. Then, at the end of the day, I ask teachers to invite students to pull their notebooks out and write down three things they are thankful for. Remember, we want them to be good at school but also good at life; ending the school day this way sets students up for success.

If you're just getting started on your gratitude journey, here are a few tips I recommend to make the most of your practice:

1. Be Consistent

Habits form out of consistency. If we're going to make this a daily practice, we want to be set up for success. As James Clear, author of *Atomic Habits: An Easy & Proven Way to Build Good Habits & Break Bad Ones*, says, "You do not rise to the level of your goals. You fall to the level of your systems."[46] To train your brain to find the best in all possible situations, practice journaling daily.

When you're ready to start practicing gratitude, you need a system in place. Ask yourself, "When am I going to do my daily gratitude? Is it going to be in the morning while I have my coffee? At night right before I go to bed?" Where or when you choose to write in your journal isn't the important part; what matters is that you make it a habit. Toward that end, Clear argues that habits should be obvious, so put your journal somewhere you will see it every day. That could be on your nightstand or by the coffee pot in the kitchen.

We don't have to be perfect with our gratitude system. I don't always do my gratitude journal on the weekends because I have a different routine. But because I've engineered my environment, built my system, and practiced gratitude consistently, on Monday I pick my gratitude journal up and start again.

2. Write It Down

Thinking gratefully is a good first step in gaining the benefits of practicing gratitude, but when we write things down, they seep into our subconscious brain a little more. And remember to be specific with your gratitude!

Keeping a gratitude journal is also a great opportunity for creativity. Find a beautiful journal that you want to open every day. Grab some fancy-schmancy colorful pens and markers. If it helps you, doodle pictures next to your list. Make it your own!

3. Feel It

We've talked about how writing down what you're grateful for is a step above just thinking about it. But if you want to really make the most of this practice, you should write down what you're grateful for *and* take a few moments to let yourself feel the gratitude. You can close your eyes and take note of how being grateful makes your body feel. Make the experience as real as possible. See the thing you are thankful for in your mind and feel the emotions that come from it. Simply writing down what you're grateful for, without experiencing it, defeats the purpose of the exercise. Make it real and it will last.

5 Gratitude Journal Prompts to Find Gratitude Today

A gratitude journal can be about so much more than listing things you're grateful for. Here are some practical tips to get you thinking with a grateful heart. Once the journal practice is part of your daily routine, you likely won't need these techniques anymore.

1. Look in the Mirror

This is your chance to truly acknowledge what you love about yourself! Do you like your eyes, your hair, your smile? Write it down and celebrate it. But then go deeper. What about your intelligence? Your strength? Your giving nature? Your ability to be a good friend? What about the hobbies you love? You are a beautiful collection of good things. Write them down and validate the goodness within you.

2. "What If _____ Was Missing from My Life?"

It's easy to say you're grateful for certain things in your life. It can be harder to articulate *why* you're so thankful for them. So, flip the script!

Ask yourself what would be different about your life if the thing you're grateful for was suddenly missing. We're talking about things like the people you love, the modern conveniences that make daily life easier, and the material possessions you hold dear. Imagine what it would be like to live without those things—and then write it down!

3. The Great Outdoors

There are things to be grateful for all around us. Finding them is as easy as stepping outside!

Take a hike and describe how the ground feels beneath your feet. Find your favorite color in a flower garden, in the treetops, in the sky above—and put the feeling it gives you into words. Spend a day in the park and make note of everything that makes you smile.

4. Gratitude at Work

Most of us spend long hours at work. So, shouldn't we look for things to be grateful for while we're there? Is it a caring principal? The comfort of a reliable paycheck? A student who hugged you today? A coworker who always has your back? Make note of all the things that make you grateful to have meaningful work in your life.

5. Get Personal

Put into words why you're so thankful for the family members and friends in your life. Explain why a recent experience meant so much to you. Describe why being a part of your community is so rewarding. Talk about your favorite book or a way to pass the time. If it means something to you personally, then it's something to be thankful for!

If you need more prompts as you work in your gratitude journal, you can also download the *Gratitude Prompt and 21-Day Tracker* from my website. It gives you (or your students) prompts for where you can look for gratitude in your life. You can use the following QR code to download it.

It's important to write in your gratitude journal for twenty-one days because the 21/90 rule states that it takes twenty-one days to make a habit and ninety days to make that habit a permanent lifestyle change.[47] This is a guideline more than a rule, but our brains like habits because they are efficient, and when a behavior becomes a habit, our brains don't have to think so hard about doing it.

Developing gratitude through journaling might seem simple—it only takes a few minutes every day to complete. But it can unlock an incredible power within us. When we start to look at everything around us in a positive way, we feel lighter, we are less stressed, we sleep better, and we are all-around healthier. This gift is not only something we can give to ourselves but something we can give to our students as well.

Chapter 7

EXERCISE DRIVES HAPPINESS

Move Your Body and Get Happy

Moving our bodies is one of the most important things we can do for our mental health, but as we've talked about in previous chapters, the teaching profession does not leave educators with a lot of time or energy to focus on their health. When teachers are coming into school early to prep, staying late to help tutor, and taking papers home to grade, going to the gym for thirty minutes a day seems like an impossible task. However, improving our physical health is critical to our happiness because our bodies are ultimately foundational for our lives. Incorporating physical fitness into our daily routines can yield astonishing benefits when it comes to emotional health.

The goal of this book is to give teachers strategies to reclaim their happiness. The tools I'm sharing are simple, but it can be hard to make them a daily practice. There is pretty clear research about what happy people do differently and about specific strategies to get there. We already talked about the power of gratitude—one of the top five happiness habits. The other top four are physical exercise, meditation, kindness, and relationships. This chapter is devoted to physical exercise and taking care of your body—a habit that most of us have had a love-hate relationship with at some point in our lives. Whether you're a body builder, an avid runner, a yoga instructor, or someone whose only exercise is walking around the playground supervising recess, this chapter is for you.

Embracing the Benefits of Bodily Movement

I first learned about the interconnectedness of bodily health and emotional health when I stumbled across the Netflix documentary *Stutz*, featuring Dr. Phil Stutz and actor Jonah Hill. In the film, Dr. Stutz's nontraditional psychotherapy changes Hill's life because it focuses on solutions rather than problems, which Stutz sees as opportunities that lead us to our untapped potential.[48]

Stutz focuses on a concept he calls the life force pyramid. Our life force, according to Stutz, is that power nestled in the deep recesses of our being, waiting to be brought to the surface from the innermost parts of ourselves.[49] It's the energetic vibration we are all made of and the spirit that lives inside us. This power is available to all of us, and when we tap into it, it moves us forward in our lives. I promise you, you have it too.

Dr. Stutz explains that the life force pyramid consists of three levels: the body, relationships, and yourself. He says that if we work to address our needs on all three levels of the pyramid, everything else falls into place, meaning our healthy habits become easier to achieve, we will feel better mentally and physically, and overall our lives will be better.[50]

The body is the base of the life force pyramid, representing our physical health. We can build this foundation by getting adequate sleep and eating foods that are good for our brains and our bodies, but I'm going to focus this chapter on physical exercise because moving your body is something almost every teacher can do to achieve more energy inside and outside the classroom.

For a lot of us, physical exercise might prompt negative emotions. Often, we think about working out to lose weight or look a certain way, but I want you to think about it in terms of helping your mental health. When we neglect our physical health, we may experience mental and emotional struggles. On the other hand, when we care for our bodies, we take a crucial step toward building a strong foundation that science proves can lead to a happier and more fulfilling life. Building exercise habits is also important because it is impactful. In fact, research shows when you move your body thirty minutes a day at least five days a week, all kinds of crazy-good stuff starts happening for you![51] Sonja Lyubomirsky focused her research on systematically observing, comparing, and experimenting on happy and unhappy people. She found the happiest participants were the ones who made physical exercise a daily habit.[52]

When we move our bodies enough, endorphins, our bodies' natural painkillers, flow freely, automatically lifting our mood. Serotonin, known as the happy chemical, is released. The antidepressant effects of exercise have also been linked to a drop in stress hormones, which, let's face it, we all could use. Exercise promotes heart health and enhances blood flow and circulation while also pumping more oxygen and nutrients to the brain.[53]

According to Dr. Lisa Mosconi, author of *The XX Brain: The Groundbreaking Science Empowering Women to Maximize Cognitive Health and Prevent Alzheimer's Disease*, "Exercise keeps our DNA young. In several studies, higher levels of exercise have been linked to a good nine fewer years of aging at the cellular level."[54] That's right. Throw away the face cream and start exercising if you want to remain nine years younger than your biological body. We can turn back the clock!

Exercise causes physical changes in our brains. Dr. Mosconi states that "study after study shows that leading an active lifestyle keeps your brain younger. On brain scans, as compared to physically active people, the sedentary ones show an acceleration of cellular aging and brain shrinkage, while also exhibiting a much higher number of Alzheimer's plaques."[55] Taken as a whole, research shows that working out regularly protects us from sickness and disease while increasing our ability to think, reason, and be in the here and now.[56] That's why exercise is one of the strategies my counselor, whom I call "the great potentializer," Charlie, used with me for years. I tended to fly off the handle and let my emotions get the better of me. When that would happen, Charlie would say, "Kim, when Scott ticks you off, go for a run before you react to him. You'll be in a better place to discuss this with him when you come back." While my husband is so laid-back that he rarely ruffles my feathers anymore, I still run every day.

As a former teacher, I know how quickly our schedules fill up and how skipping exercise feels like the easier way to get everything done. It can also feel like one more thing you have to work into your already harried schedule. But as you'll learn in subsequent chapters, there are ways for us to gain some of our time back and put it toward habits that make a huge difference in our lives. Part of the reason I'm writing this book is to show educators that we are allowed to claim time for ourselves and the things that fuel us. We do have the capability to remove things from our schedules that stress or drain us and instead shift to the habits and experiences that fuel us. This way teachers can devote energy to their students and still have a healthy life outside of the classroom.

Remember, exercise isn't about fitting into a smaller pair of pants; it's about getting into a rhythm where you are naturally getting regular physical exercise and you feel better because of it. When we get clear on how we want to feel, then we can make small improvements to our lives. I always teach people that success in any part of life is not just about the goals you want to achieve; it's more powerful to focus on *how you want to feel*. Then you can make moves that align your life with those feelings.

Getting Moving

Of course, starting an exercise routine is much easier said than done. I get it, and I can hear you thinking, "Kim, I simply don't have time to exercise." Or "Kim, I've had knee surgery and can't exercise." While I don't want to dismiss that exercising poses a challenge for many people, I must tell you about a man I met on our city greenway this past year.

Each morning when I ran on my town's local greenway, I'd see him walking. We always greeted each other with a smile as we passed. He used a walker and moved incredibly slowly, taking a step at a time while scooting his walker along with him. Yet I noticed he walked every day from when I started my run until forty-five minutes later, when I ended it.

I was in awe of what he made himself do each day. He would go up and down the greenway with great difficulty while I cruised by him on my running legs. One day I stopped and talked to him.

I learned his name, Kevin. He explained that he has spina bifida, meaning his spine didn't fuse properly when he was born. As a young child, he had braces on his legs, similar to those of Forrest Gump.

Kevin had endured knee surgeries, foot surgery, and recently a split and tethered spinal cord. Yet each morning, I would see him exercising even if it was ninety degrees or blustery and cold. He explained that he started walking in 2019 after retiring because he noticed that, especially with age combined with his condition, he was becoming less mobile. At first, he could only walk half a block before he'd have to turn around. Fast-forward to 2023 and sixty-two-year-old Kevin walks four miles a day with his walker! He said it takes about two hours, but he's dedicated to his physical health.

I thought about how many people would have walked half a block, felt the way Kevin did, and then stopped trying. I think I might have given up too.

I think about all the times we make excuses for not being able to do something. Too many times, we use age as an excuse to no longer thrive

in our lives. Yes, the body and brain decline with age, but you can get fitter and healthier at fifty-five and sixty than you were at forty-five, and you can remain physically fit and cognitively sharp well into your seventies and eighties.

Even for those of us who stay active, moving our bodies in helpful new ways can be a challenge. As much as I hesitate to say this, for all the eye rollers out there, I love running. I run forty miles a week and I rarely miss a day; I have always been a runner. Even though I have a consistent and fulfilling running routine, though, I can find myself not feeling my best. That's when I know I need to make a change.

This happened recently. I knew that to succeed in changing, I was going to need help, so I hired Jess Sheehan, a health and fitness coach that I met while keynoting at her school in Hauppauge, New York. I had been following Jess on Instagram (@sheehanbyrnefit), watching how she trains athletes as well as normal people like me on everything from creating stronger bodies to eating clean and establishing a healthy lifestyle.

I told Jess that while I'm the girl who runs every single day of the week, no matter what, my body wasn't shifting, I wanted to take a nap every afternoon, and I felt the midlife woman's stomach creeping on. Jess gently suggested I replace three of my running days with two whole-body strength-training workouts and one rest day.

I'm telling you this story because I did not want to have to change. I like running and having my routine; it's easy and I don't have to think much about it. I was comfortable. My brain and body resisted much of what Jess was telling me to do. After twenty years of running every single day, just the idea of taking one day a week off made me anxious.

For the first few weeks, I felt depressed. Every Saturday I would go down to my basement, get on FaceTime with Jess, and she would coach me through a workout. As my body flailed around on the floor like a circus clown, I couldn't help but feel inadequate. I was terrible at the exercises she was having me do because I had overworked certain parts of my body for years and completely neglected others. During the first several workouts, I cried—multiple times.

But guess what? I stuck with it, and slowly but surely, I rewired my brain and body connection. Muscles that hadn't been firing and talking to my brain in a long time started firing again. Yes, it was hard.

Yes, I hated it at times. But now that I've proved to my brain that I can change my exercise habits, I can say it seems to be worth it.

I believe we can do hard things. We can do more than we think we can. We can climb another mountain. We can push ourselves, and usually when we do, it's worth it. We must be willing to make ourselves uncomfortable to grow, and growing is so important no matter our age. Remember, every time we exchange the couch and chowing down on chips while watching Netflix (also a favorite hobby of mine) for lacing up our tennis shoes and going for a walk, we receive a positive benefit to our minds, bodies, and spirits.

Look, if we truly want to live better lives, we have to start doing things differently. We can't say we want to be happier, less stressed, and more energetic if we keep doing the same things we were doing before. This doesn't mean you must have the strength to upend all your bad habits, but it does mean you have to start adding better habits into your life.

The hardest part is just getting started. Once you get started, suddenly those struggles and excuses that kept you on the couch will float away. Here are my five tips for getting started.

How to Get Started with Exercise

1. Decide on an Activity

Dance, do yoga, walk, run, bike, stretch, swim, strength train, hula-hoop? The important part is not what we do to move; it's that we *are* moving and having fun!

2. Put It on the Calendar

Schedule exercise in your calendar. Remember, when we make something ritualistic, our brains begin to take on the identity of a person who performs these actions. Then they become a natural part of our routines and everyday lives. Maybe it's stretching right after you get out of bed or taking a walk as soon as you get home from work.

3. Start Small

In an ideal world, we'd exercise for thirty minutes at least five times a week. The research says this is optimal. When you're first getting started, it's okay to do less. Start with one workout class or a quick walk around your neighborhood. If you can't do thirty minutes, begin with fifteen minutes and gradually increase.

4. Just Start!

Make it happen. Decide right now who you want to be and how you want to feel. The decisions we're making right now are determining our quality of life as well as how we'll feel in our sixties, seventies, and eighties.

A lot of information in this chapter is probably stuff we've all heard before. A lot of us have struggled to take this advice and find the motivation and time to move our bodies. It's hard work—trust me, I know. But if we want to be happier, healthier, and stronger for our students, we have to put in the work. Each time you go for a bike ride or dance for thirty minutes with your kids, remember Phil Stutz's foundation of the life force pyramid that helps you get unstuck not only in your body but also in your mind. Incorporating physical exercise into your routine is laying down the crucial foundation for feeling better, living long, and being happier.

Chapter 8

THE ALIGNED HEART

Nurturing Happiness through Relationships

We need connections with others and to feel seen, heard, and valued. As Brené Brown says, "We are wired for connection. It's in our biology. From the time we are born, we need connections to thrive emotionally, physically, spiritually, and intellectually."[57] Daniel Goleman, psychologist and author of *Social Intelligence: The New Science of Human Relationships*, concurs. He's discovered groundbreaking evidence in biology and brain science which reveals that we are "wired to connect" and that relationships have a meaningful impact on our lives. Goleman finds that human connection shapes our brains and affects cells throughout our bodies, down to the level of our genes.[58]

It's no surprise, then, that the second level of the life force pyramid, according to Dr. Stutz, is relationships.[59] Other researchers place a similar focus on our lives with other people as integral to our emotional health. According to Sonja Lyubomirsky, "One of the strongest findings in the literature on happiness is that happy people have better relationships than do their less happy peers. Happy people have strong marriages, friendships, and families that they count on."[60]

Why then do we pull away from others, especially in times of struggle? Self-isolating is counterintuitive to what we need during hard times: support from our people. We need people who can listen and reassure us, help us solve problems, offer emotional intimacy, act as confidants, and share problems. We must be intentional with our relationships because, on the other hand, some relationships are toxic, emotionally draining, and unhealthy, which is where we draw on what we discussed in chapter 11. Despite those risks, though, because we are wired to connect, building strong, healthy relationships is also integral for emotional health.

Relationships: What Are They Good For?

Great thinkers have long understood the importance of friendship. The Greek philosopher Epicurus, who lived two thousand years ago, is known for his philosophy of simple pleasures and friendship. He eloquently explained, "Of all the things that wisdom provides for living one's entire life in happiness, the greatest by far is the possession of friendship."[61] Therefore, it is no surprise that positive psychologists Ed Diener and Martin Seligman have found that strong interpersonal characteristics are the best predictors of life satisfaction and happiness.[62]

Research goes beyond just saying that friendships support happiness; studies show that having strong relationships can actually lengthen our life-span—even more than quitting smoking.[63] In *The How of Happiness*, Sonja Lyubomirsky discusses a study that analyzed three communities of long-living people—Sardinians in Italy, Okinawans in Japan, and Seventh-day Adventists in Loma Linda, California. What was at the top of the list of their commonalities? Putting family first and being socially engaged.[64]

When we cultivate important relationships in our lives, with family or friends, we begin to experience more positive emotions. Lyubomirsky's research focuses on how happy people behave and habitually engage in their lives. She found that "happy people devote a great amount of time to their family and friends, nurturing and enjoying those relationships."[65] Studies on friendship also point to benefits like boosting immunity and reducing the risk of depression.[66]

The happiness we experience from relationships is also surprisingly robust. Remember hedonic adaptation, the ability to adjust quickly to any circumstances? It explains why when we make more money or lose weight, we are happier for a hot minute, and then we make an emotional adjustment. Interestingly, the happiness that comes from our relationships with family and friends is buffered from hedonic adaptation, so these relationships create a whammo of a long-term benefit.[67]

We all have a human need for connection and to be relational because we were designed with that need. Unfortunately, in today's world, it seems like we're seeing less and less of this need being met. People used to spend time sitting on their porches, chatting with neighbors, attending neighborhood BBQs, or taking a few minutes to catch up with an old friend while they shopped for groceries. But with the raggedy roadrunner race of life, people are more isolated than they've ever been, and they have less time for these types of connections.

Unfortunately, the absence of friendship also has dire consequences. Surgeon General Dr. Vivek H. Murthy has gone so far as to say that "loneliness is far more than just a bad feeling—it harms both individual and societal health. It is associated with a greater risk of cardiovascular disease, dementia, stroke, depression, anxiety, and premature death."[68] These risks led the surgeon general to release a report that characterizes loneliness as an outright "epidemic."

Investing in Marriage and Partnership

Marriages and partnerships are integral to our understanding of how relationships affect happiness. Significant others are special relationships in our lives because we spend so much of our time with them, making decisions together and leaning on each other when things get hard. Healthy relationships and strong social bonds create emotional intimacy and are of great benefit, especially when we're going through times of stress, disappointment, or struggle. Research shows that people who have strong social support are healthier and live longer. It's also been shown that intimate relationships are a bit immune to hedonic adaptation, which makes them all the more special.[69]

Ninety percent of adults end up marrying, but almost half of all marriages end in divorce, while 67 percent of second marriages end in Splitsville.[70] Thankfully, I still fall in the 40 percent of second marriages that make it. We are in year twenty-one and still going. Whew!

Drs. John and Julie Gottman, a married couple, run The Gottman Institute as marriage researchers. They have conducted research on all facets of relationships over the last five decades and can predict with 91 percent accuracy which couples will stay together and which will divorce. In their work, the Gottmans have found that an important contributor to happy couples is time: couples that end up happy together spend a lot of time talking. Happy couples spend five hours more per week being together and talking than couples that don't make it.[71]

Yes, I know now you think I'm asking you to find another five hours a week to dedicate to your marriage. If you're like me and you're an empty nester, you have the time. If you still have kids running around and it's the funny farm at your house, I suggest you start small because, remember, small changes still create a ripple effect.

Developing a commitment to communication with your partner might be as simple as expressing gratitude to them more frequently or complimenting them, which takes seconds. I know my husband's love language is words of affirmation, and even though I have often felt like I give him many compliments, I've had to amp that up in our relationship because he needs triple the dose compared to the average human—and I'm willing to do it to make him feel loved. Even small gestures help. For example, my husband and I started a new routine after reading the Gottmans' research: we start each day with a fifteen-second hug. The Gottmans' research suggests thirty seconds, but fifteen seems sufficient to us. It's now part of our everyday routine. A hug in the morning and definitely one at the end of the day have become daily habits.

Think about how you might start small, and if I can push you on this, I would also suggest a nonnegotiable date night at least every other week. This doesn't have to involve going out to dinner and a movie. A date night is just about spending intentional time with one another. It could just mean taking some snacks out on the porch and spending some one-on-one time talking. That will do wonders for your marriage and help you remember that you are more than a parent, teacher, etc.

Friendships, in and out of the Classroom

When we connect with people, share our burdens, and celebrate our successes, we create intimacy and experience more love, which happens to be the most happiness-inducing emotion there is. When we experience more love, we feel happier and more satisfied with life.[72]

I must admit, though, that friendships are the social connections that I struggle with the most. My marriage is strong because I've spent years investing time into that relationship. But when it comes to spending time with friends, I feel like I could be better. Yes, from time to time, I get together with friends, and there are people who I text with often, but I know from the research that I need to be more intentional about making regular time for friends—not just every other month.

Again the most important strategy for creating stronger friendships involves dedicating intentional time to others. You can do this by creating rituals or consistent plans with friends. Maybe it's a monthly dinner date, meeting up at the gym, or texting daily.

As teachers, we spend a lot of time at school surrounded by our fellow educators. I think it's safe to say that for many educators, their closest friends are their colleagues. We often build connections by eating together, serving recess duty together, or giggling together about an inside joke at a staff meeting. These relationships may begin by circumstance, but they also can be vitally important to our happiness.

Individual teachers need to realize the value of collegial friendships, and it is also important for leaders to recognize that value so that they can build capacity in work environments that foster positive relationships. By building meaningful relationships with the people we spend so much of our day with, we will have more energy to devote to students, and we'll be more excited to go to work.

When I was a fourth-grade teacher, the administrators worked hard to cultivate a supportive and familial environment. Our assistant superintendent and superintendent walked around hand delivering gifts to each of the teachers every December, personally thanking them for their hard work. I was given a lot of encouragement because they placed books in my hands that helped me further my exploration of being a great teacher. Also, Mary, the superintendent, would place little note cards with heartfelt messages in our mailboxes throughout the year with quotes reminding us of our greatness and contribution to others.

These small gestures made a big difference. Every member of the staff could feel like they were valued. These acts also backed up the claims our administration made about teachers being part of their family. Every person had their needs met. Even after I left the school corporation, I remember hearing about a teacher who was struggling to support his family. In the summer he took a physically demanding job in a factory to make ends meet. When the administrators heard, they worked to create a position in the summer school program so he could leave the factory and still support his family.

Since the administrators set the precedent that everyone in the building was valued and important, teachers treated each other with kindness and, from that, many meaningful relationships blossomed. I remember the atmosphere of the school being uplifting and positive, and because of that, everyone was able to show up in a more nurturing way for their students.

Random Acts of Kindness

Happy people also tend to perform kind, good-hearted acts for others. In fact, a 2010 Harvard Business School survey of happiness in 136 countries found that altruistic people—in this case, people who were generous financially, such as with charitable donations—were happiest overall.[73]

Here again, the relationship between kindness and happiness comes down, in part, to physiology. Kindness stimulates the production of serotonin. This feel-good chemical heals your wounds, calms you down, and makes you happy. One study found that 50 percent of participants had more energy and felt calmer and less depressed after helping someone else.[74] Even just seeing someone do something nice for someone else releases oxytocin in our brain. This compound, sometimes referred to as the love hormone, helps make us more confident and improves our health.[75]

This phenomenon is sometimes referred to as the *helper's high*. It means we feel good when we help someone out even if we don't get anything return.[76] I find it easy to practice this happiness habit. It can be as simple as thanking the Walmart cashier for getting you through the bagging line quickly. Trust me, when you've had panic disorder, you are super appreciative of this.

Or the other day I had an army veteran as my cashier, and I just took the time to connect with him. I said, "I see your hat and that you're an army veteran, and so is my dad. Which war did you serve in?" He proceeded to tell me about being in World War II in Germany. This conversation led to him telling me he lost his wife eight years ago and how much he misses her (and her home cooking). When I drove my cart away from his register, he said, "Ma'am, it's been real nice talking to you. I wish you blessings." Small acts like this mean the world to someone else—and the beauty is not only do they make other people feel good, but they make us feel good too.

As I alluded to above, my previous superintendent, Mary, was the world's greatest at random acts of kindness, both big and small. She always took time to make sure the teachers in all three schools (elementary, middle, and high) knew they were valued and appreciated. Every so often she'd include a candy bar and a handwritten note telling you something specific she had noticed you'd done. Fifteen years later I hired her to be my editor for this book, and we met for lunch to discuss it. She arrived with the same style of pop-up quote card, which took me right back to working for her years ago.

Here's an example of another random act of kindness from her that I've never forgotten. When I graduated from college, there weren't many teaching jobs available. Crazy, I know. When I went to work at Perry Central Community Schools, where Mary was the superintendent, I was hired as an assistant for Lights-On, which was the after-school program. My hourly rate was eight dollars. Mary held the highest position in the district, and she knew that I was a struggling single mom, so she figured out a way to take my pay rate to fifteen dollars an hour within the first year. To this day, I've never forgotten what that meant to me.

Another great way to practice random acts of kindness is to start your day by sending an email or text thanking or complimenting someone you know. It only takes a minute, so try it right now. Take your phone out and send a text to someone telling them one of three things:

1. Your favorite thing about them
2. Something about them for which you are thankful
3. A compliment

And just see what happens!

Being intentional about kindness comes naturally to some of us and not so much for others. It's so easy to get lost in the harried world of our lives that it can feel like another chore. But these acts don't have to be large. They can be small acts performed within the scope of what we're already doing. But when we think about them as acts of kindness or take a little extra effort or time to help someone out, we get a happiness kickback. Try donating blood, helping a student after school, visiting an elderly family member, writing a thank-you note, smiling at the person walking by—or remembering the simple checkout or text message examples. When we are kind to others or help them, we find ourselves connecting. When we see others happy because of something we've done, our own lives begin to improve.

Chapter 9

MINIMUM EFFECTIVE DOSE

Unraveling the Myth of Overwork

The hamster wheel of life keeps us in a "hustle mindset" more often than not. We know we need to get off the wheel, but we don't know how. Teachers and school leaders are especially vulnerable to feeling like they need to be working all the time. Educators feel like the key to being less busy is letting go of responsibilities or caring less, but teachers can't let go without hurting their students.

We want to do what's best for every student, so we agree to stay after school to tutor. Instead of stopping for lunch, we grade papers at our desks, stuffing bites of leftover pizza in our mouths as we flip to the next paper. We skip a girls' night to read student essays, and we agree to a Saturday workshop instead of spending time with our families. It's a to-do list that is impossible to get to the bottom of.

As a fourth-grade teacher, I always felt like I was being asked to add more things to my plate. It wasn't anyone's fault; it's just the state of the current education system and the demands that keep piling on everyone who works within that system. Among those recent additions, social-emotional learning is paramount, but how are we supposed to find the extra minutes in the day to teach these very important lessons? Am I supposed to skimp on the history lesson that needs to be covered in depth? Even though I haven't had my own classroom for a while, I never want to forget what it felt like to try meeting these constant demands. If this describes your own experience in the classroom, I see you.

Everyone knows the expression "Less is more." We yearn to do less, but we don't know how or where to even begin. The real problem isn't that we can't decide how to cut back, but rather that nothing is ever taken off teachers' plates. No one ever says, "Kim, we need you to incorporate social-emotional learning into your curriculum, and to do so, you are now only responsible for eighteen of the thirty-four math standards for your grade level."

Remember in an earlier chapter when I said, "We may not be able to change the system, but we can change how we operate within the system?" While hustle culture is a broader phenomenon, educators are especially overworked, and it can feel hard for them to take things off their plate without worrying students will pay the price. Educators need strategies for deducing how to lessen their workload without feeling like they're making sacrifices.

The Problems with Hustle Culture

Hustle culture is prevalent in this world. We operate within workplaces and homes that require hard work and long hours to arrive at the success that will make us feel like worthwhile humans. When we think of being busy, we think of being productive. However, recent research has demonstrated that this equation may not be as accurate as we think.

In fact, at some point our tendency to hustle yields diminishing returns. In his work on management and productivity, author Jack Nevison looked at several different studies on productivity and the number of hours employees worked. Overall, that research found that employees who worked over fifty hours a week only really did thirty-seven hours' worth of work. Employees who worked up to fifty-five hours a week got even less work done. Nevison calls this principle the *Rule of Fifty*: every hour over fifty that you work in a week makes you less productive.[77]

THE RULE OF 50

⟶ After 50 hours there's no productivity gain for the extra time worked.

In fact, it goes *backward*.

⟶ 50 hours produces 37 hours of useful work

⟶ At 55 hours, that drops down to 30

The more hours we work, the more stressed our brains become. Remember, when we're stressed, we cannot access certain parts of our brain—the parts that truly make us productive. As Shawn Achor's research suggests, "A positive brain is 31% more productive than a brain at negative, neutral, or stressed."[78]

When the brain is stressed, we do things like shop online for things we don't need, or we click on our social media fifteen times because we're exhausted and think we're giving our brains a quick break. These actions lead us to be less productive overall.

This is a no-brainer to most of you, but the reality is that sometimes we don't know how to turn the spigot off. We all get turned around in our responsibilities and priorities, and sometimes, we just don't know what to do.

As teachers, our work doesn't end when the last child files out at the end of the school day. We spend hours upon hours prepping, perfecting lesson plans, entering grades, keeping our inboxes cleaned out, and staying up to date on the latest instructional methods.

Teachers are sacrificing everything from their personal time to their sanity. Worst of all, this extra work and worrying doesn't guarantee the results we want to see. In fact, it often leads to major burnout. The bottom line is we think we're being productive when we're working long hours, but we're not. The more hours you work, the less effectively you are operating.

We see Nevison's Rule of Fifty in classrooms every day. A few years ago, I was providing professional development to a school when a teacher friend asked to speak to me in the hallway. She was upset and said she had decided at the beginning of the year that she wasn't going to put in all the long hours and weekends at school. She told me she'd spent the year before missing her first grader's soccer games on Saturdays because she was at school all day prepping for the next week.

This teacher then told me that she always receives Highly Effective ratings on her yearly evaluations (Indiana's highest ranking), but this year she received a rating of Effective. "I guess I need to go back to spending weeknights and weekends in my classroom," she said with a sigh. "I let myself slip this year."

We had to have a heart-to-heart conversation. First, I told this teacher that she had a right to take back her evenings and her weekends. No one should be forced to miss their child's games because there's more work to do. She shouldn't *dare* go back to sacrificing time spent supporting her child to toil away in the classroom during her rightful time off.

I knew it was time for this teacher to set boundaries. I told her, "Perhaps if this is the case and what is required to be rated Highly Effective, you have to ask yourself if it's really worth it." I asked, "What kind of pain hurts the most? Does it hurt more to know your so-called rating is 'Effective' this year? Or does it pain you more to miss adequate family time after school and your children's sporting events?" Three years later this same teacher emailed me and said, "I can't believe how much that conversation with you helped me. I am less focused on the words 'highly effective' and more focused on the benefits I have gained from getting more of my life back outside of teaching. It feels so good to know my weekends are mine and my family's again. I'm never going back to the crazy overworking again. It's simply not worth it."

This teacher's story resonates with experiences at all levels of educational employment. John, a school principal from Texas, told me, "Kim, up until this year, I have existed solely for the purpose of building my school. The crux of it is the more you give, the more they want, demand, and extort."

Thankfully, John seems to have turned a corner. "I have come to realize that my family matters too," he told me. "I have missed so many milestones for kids and my family. Not that my work isn't important. It is. But I have now decided it's time to give myself some grace."

Minimum Effective Dosage: The Cure for Overwork

I've spent much of my life feeling like I'm a valuable human being only if I've hustled all day, accomplished a ton of tasks, and wearily walked myself out of the school building (or now my office) in the evening. But why am I not just as valuable when I don't pull a ten-hour workday? Am I less than because I worked four hours that day and decided my body needed rest, a nap, or a visit with my hundred-year-old grandmother?

As teachers especially, it can feel hard to know when we can stop working and direct our energy toward other areas of our lives. I've found Tim Ferriss's concept of the minimum effective dose (MED) incredibly helpful for finding that stopping point. In *The 4-Hour Workweek*, Ferriss defines MED as "the smallest dose that will provide the desired outcome." Anything beyond MED, Ferriss says, is wasteful.[79]

MED can be hard to conceptualize, so let's use spaghetti as an example. When I make spaghetti, I toss the noodles in the water and boil them at around 212 degrees Fahrenheit. This softens the noodles just enough. Now, I could boil those noodles at 242 degrees or 265 degrees, but noodles are noodles, and they aren't going to taste better just because you boil them at a higher temperature. In fact, turning up the heat might make them sticky and mushy. It's not like putting noodles in the pan and boiling them beyond 212 degrees will produce a chocolate cake with vanilla icing, my favorite dessert, so why turn the heat up more than the directions say?

MED is the law of diminishing returns, which is a principle that states the advantages obtained from a particular thing will decrease proportionally as more effort or energy is invested in it. This means we have to set boundaries and adhere to them. In the noodle analogy, the bottom line is that the higher temperatures would only consume more heat, water, and resources that could be used productively elsewhere. The MED is 212 degrees.

Yet I see teachers and school leaders turning up the heat on their lives and getting burned out without any benefits.

I always explain the MED concept when doing my "Science of Happiness" keynote. One time after that presentation, a teacher came up to me and said, "Kim Strobel, I think you are crazy, but I'm going to put this to the test. I'm going to get out the door almost every day by four o'clock this year and see what happens."

Two years later, I got an email from her. "I cannot believe I'm reporting this, but you have changed my life. After learning about the Minimum Effective Dosage from you, I set myself up to be my own private study on this concept. I chose to work normal workweeks and get home to my family. Somehow, I am getting most of it done and I don't know how but it's working! I am more productive and able to complete everything while still having time left over for my family. Thank you."

Given that teacher's transformation, we have to ask ourselves: How much more effective could you be if you spent less time in the classroom after the bell rings? Yes, I know extra time is sometimes necessary; that's just a fact of life. There are times I still pull sixty- to seventy-hour workweeks, and I wish I could report differently. But when I start to get into the cycle of overworking, I step back, analyze if hustle is helping, and correct course. It's not easy, but it's always worth it.

Each teacher needs to figure out their MED and then know when to stop. We have to recognize when putting in overtime is making a difference and when we're doing it out of guilt, worry, or misplaced obligation.

I know teachers are ready to quit "overboiling their water." I know teachers would prefer to get out the door by 4:00 p.m., and now I am encouraging you to do it! Yes, it's going to cause anxiety. Yes, it's going to feel uncomfortable. Your brain is not used to this. You're accustomed to getting everything done. You are used to striving for perfection. But we must push ourselves and learn to optimize our time. And school leaders, I'd love it if you could model this behavior to normalize it for your teachers.

We are allowed to reclaim the other parts of our lives. A retired teacher was volunteering at a school where I was providing professional development. She came up to me and said, "Kim, I know you work with teachers all across the country. I am someone who stayed each evening until six o'clock or later and worked too much as a teacher. When I look back, I would do anything to have that time back with my babies. Tell those teachers to go home to their families. It's the best piece of advice I can give them as someone who has lived this."

In the moment it feels like we have to work hard to set our students up for success, but what our students deserve is a teacher who is not exhausted, guilt-ridden, and overworked. It might feel like getting those essays graded by the end of the week is the most important thing, but no student will remember or care if the grade comes in on Friday or Monday. Students will remember the teacher, who came into school every morning with a smile and shared stories about their family and their life. Teachers deserve to take a step back and be fulfilled in every aspect of their lives, and students deserve that too.

Chapter 10

RADICAL WELLNESS

The Self-Care Nobody Is Talking About

I have struggled with *self-care* as a word and a concept. Now, more than ever, it seems people need self-care. Increasing pressures at work and home have caused so many people to feel burned out that the World Health Organization has declared a global mental health crisis.[80]

We are constantly hearing sound bites about self-care that are not at all what I consider it to be. "Take five deep breaths. Eat something healthy. Rub some lavender oil on your wrist. Walk one lap around the school and come back in."

The biggest problem with self-care is that it's marketed as something that's going to help people, when at best it's going to make them feel good for a few minutes. People talk about self-care like it will solve all their problems, but it won't. This is particularly troubling for educators because they really are struggling with heavy workloads and mental health issues, and the media or well-intentioned people are telling them that when they learn to "take care of themselves," they will get their lives back. I wish it were that easy, but it's not.

Self-care promoted in this way also causes guilt because teachers are told this is one more thing they're supposed to figure out, but no one is telling them how to find the time for it. These superficial self-care tactics only avoid the real issues teachers are facing, making teachers feel even more behind. As Laura Arenella recently shared in our Teach Happy Facebook group, "Mostly what teachers need is time. Self-care doesn't accomplish anything on our to-do list. There are still parent contacts, planning, grading, data record keeping, bulletin boards, report cards, classroom organization, copies, fixing the copier, continued professional development and so on. As teachers we already shortchange our families so it feels like when someone is asking us to practice self-care, it's stealing even more time from our families." Laura hit the nail on the head here, and I'm sure many of you are nodding.

Which is why this chapter is going to be crucial yet a bit challenging. I am flipping the script on self-care and showing you exactly how to carve out and create more time for you—but in ways you aren't used to. Once you learn to make these moves, this will be a game changer for you. It's time we get to the root of what's getting in our way.

Self-care isn't about eating a sweet treat or doing a face mask. These quick fixes don't change future outcomes or conquer stress and the feeling of being overwhelmed. I speak with teachers who tell me they can't wait until Friday because then they can relax, watch TV, or take a bath. Those plans are nice, and they might provide a short break from the exhaustion of the week, but they don't get to the root problem and don't change the underlying issues. You go right back to your feelings of stress and burnout. You haven't taken the necessary steps to intentionally make decisions that free up more space for you to breathe in your life.

As I have continued to read and ponder the topic, I have moved to a new phrase for self-care: *radical wellness*. Radical wellness is radical because it doesn't come naturally to us and it's really hard. It's messy and uncomfortable, and it pushes us to make decisions that put us first in the equation of our lives. Prioritizing ourselves like that requires a shift in our thinking. Radical wellness doesn't put something else on our plates, which is what we're used to; instead, it entails reframing our view of the world to see how we can better contribute by being our best selves. Being our best selves means living meaningful lives and making the world a better place. It means being our best for ourselves but also for those around us. When we can step into our best selves, we begin to own and share our light with others. We reach inside ourselves and do the inner hard work so we can emerge with a strength of character and purpose that makes a positive impact on others. We must constantly grow ourselves, as Oprah says, "To fulfill the highest expression of yourself as a human being." For teachers, this means we take care of our mental and physical health so we can feel fulfilled and joyful inside and outside the classroom.

Typical ideas about self-care don't go far enough to address teachers' needs. Instead of adding self-care regimens to their already packed schedules, educators should work to establish radical wellness by paying closer attention to meeting the real needs of their minds and bodies and taking positive steps to meet those needs.

Three Misconceptions about Self-Care

I want to take readers on the journey of how I moved from self-care to radical wellness. First, I'll talk about what self-care isn't. To do that, let's explore three of the biggest cultural myths about self-care.

1. Doing a Face Mask and Taking a Bubble Bath Is Self-Care

Self-care has become a marketing buzzword used by corporations to convince us to buy face masks, bath bombs, and lavender-scented candles. But a hydrating face mask isn't going to cure our anxiety; a pedicure isn't going to solve our problems; a hot, lavender-scented bath doesn't wipe away our never-ending to-do list; and a bottomless pitcher of margaritas on a Friday night, albeit quite enjoyable at the time, isn't going to make our jobs less hard come Monday morning. We need to stop telling teachers to take up yoga or have a spa day. Yes, these things are nice and we enjoy them, but they are only superficial self-care.

2. Self-Care Is Selfish

We are not selfish for putting ourselves first. Yep, I said it. Putting ourselves first doesn't mean we are selfish, and it doesn't mean we are neglecting others.

For a lot of people, especially women, this is the hardest part of self-care. I remember working with a group of teachers in Kentucky and asking the twenty-six women in the training to share one thing they had done for themselves over the summer. None of them could come up with a single thing. They talked about running their kids to practices, cleaning out closets, organizing the storage room, and trying to catch up on all the things they couldn't get done during the school year. They had not made any time for themselves, which was shocking to them and to me.

I'm sure these teachers were like me when I was teaching, using summer to catch up on everything neglected during the school year and getting ready for the next year. I remember how in mid-July, I would go to the grocery store and buy thirty pounds of ground beef to fry up and freeze to ease evening meal planning during the school year. This was part of my "get ready to go back to work" routine.

We know that women's roles in the workforce have grown considerably over time, which means we have a choice to make: either we keep doing it all and feel angry, resentful, tired, and ticked off a lot of the time, or we have the hard conversations with our partners where we ask for help. I chose the latter, and my husband is a whiz at many domestic chores now.

In the 1980s, sociologists Arlene Kaplan Daniels and Arlie Hochschild gave us language for these inequities in Eve's book.[81] Below are some of the key terms.

Mental Load: Mental load refers to all the thoughts in your head that keep your life and your family's lives running smoothly. This could be the three hundred lists you have whirling in your head right now, keeping track of when to buy more laundry detergent, what groceries are running low, what bills need to be paid, what maintenance needs to be scheduled, what medical appointments are coming up, when you need to line up a dog sitter for vacation, etc.

Second Shift: Second shift is the domestic work you do at home. These are the tasks that you have to complete every day, even after a long day of work. Think prepping the kids' lunches, making breakfast, making sure homework is complete, fixing dinner, straightening up the living room, mopping the kitchen floor, unloading and reloading the dishwasher, letting the dogs out, washing the sheets, and doing the grocery shopping.

Emotional Labor: Emotional labor is the work you put into making sure the relationships in your life and your family's lives are being maintained. This often includes remembering family members' birthdays, breaking up arguments, reaching out to in-laws, soothing an upset child, or sacrificing your wants and needs to make everyone else happy.

Invisible Work: Invisible work refers to the unglamorous, underappreciated tasks that caretakers do for their families without any thanks. (Remember my refrigerator story? This is the work that gets done that rarely is noticed.)

These ideas about gendered labor inequality resonate with teachers who are women. So, one potential reason female teachers might not have time for self-care is that they're trying to do it all. But the truth is that all of us, especially teachers, are prone to caring for others and not putting ourselves first. Educators spend their whole day putting their students first and not thinking about what they need. This is hard to turn off even when they go home at the end of the day.

The first step in practicing self-care is acknowledging that it's okay to prioritize ourselves. Most of us have heard the saying "You can't pour from an empty cup." I take it a step further and say our cup better be overflowing at times so that when we pour some out for others, we still have plenty for ourselves.

When we decide to put ourselves first, we become better people and better teachers. Prioritizing our own needs brings out the best in us. It's natural in the beginning to feel guilty for focusing on our own needs. But taking good care of ourselves means the people in our lives get the best of us, rather than what is left over.

3. I Don't Have Time

One of the biggest reasons people don't practice self-care is because they don't feel they have time. And the reality is that we may *not* have time in our day if we keep doing things the way we are doing them. I fall into this trap too. I told myself for the last seven years that I didn't have time to write a book. It's not that I didn't have time; it's that I wasn't prioritizing writing.

You still might be saying, "I really don't have any time." But everything we do is about making choices. Picking up our phones and scrolling through social media is an easy choice, and I enjoy it, too, but it eats away at our time—just check the screen time analytics on your phone. (Go to Settings, scroll down to Screen Time, look where it shows your daily average and click See All App & Website Activity. Prepare to be astounded). If you have it turned on, it shows you how many minutes you spent text messaging, scrolling Facebook or Instagram, and checking emails. Making time for ourselves and doing something healthy is a much harder choice than scrolling, but we still have to do it!

The next time you spend forty-five minutes scrolling Facebook, perhaps think about swapping that time out tomorrow for a thirty-minute walk around your neighborhood to get that physical exercise in.

Screens are not the only things eating up our free time. Take a few moments today to think about how you spend your time. Where can you cut out habits and replace them with more intentional self-care? Maybe being intentional with your time means waking up when your alarm first goes off instead of hitting snooze—that way, you can take thirty minutes doing something that makes you feel good. If you spend a lot of time commuting, it could mean finding a way to incorporate self-care into drive time, like listening to a book or favorite podcast.

It has become normal for everyone to be overwhelmingly busy all the time. Teachers come in early to prepare for the day, they stay late prepping the next day's lessons, and they attend workshops and conferences. We are busy, but that doesn't mean we don't have time to take care of ourselves.

Moving toward Radical Wellness

The overall problem with "self-care" is that the typically recommended practices do not get at the heart of the issues we face. True self-care is about listening to your mind and your body and seeing what they need. Often what we need isn't something glamorous. By seeing what self-care is not, we can move beyond cliché notions to specific actions that can bring radical wellness into our lives.

Radical wellness is about making actual changes to your life that are going to improve your health, create good habits, and manage your emotions. When you implement radical wellness, even though at first it might be hard, you are setting yourself up for success by pushing yourself to grow. For teachers, this might look like waking up early to go to the gym, saying no to volunteer duties, investing in therapy, or devoting a small part of your evenings to meditating. At first, you might feel worse. You could be tired from waking up earlier or feel guilty for not being more helpful. But if you stay committed to yourself, you will eventually start to see the radical improvements you are making to your life.

Simone Biles demonstrated radical wellness at the 2020 Tokyo Olympics by pulling herself out of the competition. This sparked a lot of backlash in the media because she was favored to win, but Biles was in tune with her mental health and knew what she needed to do.[82] My hope is that you start to listen to your intuition along with your body and mind to make courageous moves in your life.

Radical wellness is uncomfortable and messy, and it requires us to examine our lives from the inside out. It is not a random, long-overdue pampering with a facial or a walk in the park, and it is not a last resort; we shouldn't wait for life to come tumbling down before we become intentional with this practice. Radical wellness should be deliberate and scheduled so that it becomes a part of who you are, a habit. Radical wellness means restructuring our lives with the understanding that we deserve to feel good physically and emotionally and that those around us—our students, our families, our colleagues—need us to be our best selves.

Radical wellness is radical because it means saying no so we can say yes; it means aligning our actions with our values, even when we have to disappoint someone. Radical wellness is radical because it means we replace old belief systems with new ones so we can pave the way for well-being. In that light, radical wellness is also controversial because we will fight with ourselves to make our new beliefs the norm.

5 Steps to Incorporating Radical Wellness

Radical wellness is going to look different for everyone, but there are still concrete steps we can all take to work toward it.

1. Brainstorm Radical Wellness Practices Specific to You

Before we can get started with radical wellness, we have to take a step back and evaluate our lives. Which aspects of your life leave you feeling the most drained? When do you feel the least like yourself?

After this exercise, you might realize that getting after-work drinks with your coworkers and complaining about your boss is making you dislike your job. It might be time to stop attending happy hour and spend that time doing something that makes you feel good. For example, I stopped eating lunch in the teachers' lounge. I know that sounds awful, but it seemed like everyone was complaining, and I left feeling even more down about my job.

There are things we just can't stop doing. For instance, house chores must be done. If keeping the house clean is starting to feel like a burden, though, try asking other people in your house to help out (especially your kids or spouse), or you could try making your cleaning routine more positive by listening to happy music while you do it. Each of us knows our own routines and triggers. I know teacher salaries are tight, but maybe hiring a housecleaner to come once a month would give you something to look forward to and take a little off your plate.

Now that we've thought about the things that don't bring us joy, let's think about the things that do. Think of an activity that lights you up but that you haven't had time for. What projects are you excited about? Which part of your routine leaves you feeling better?

Maybe you love cooking but have gotten in the habit of ordering out. If you love talking with people but live alone, it might be time to start a book club or call friends on the phone. I love having time each night to chase my dogs around the house and play with them. It brings me a lot of joy and is a great way to end a stressful day.

To practice radical wellness, each of us has to determine the activities that can help us reclaim our inner peace and happiness. Radical wellness is very personal. Here are some practices you might consider, and you can likely add many other ideas to this list:

- Exercise or move your body on a regular basis.

We've already learned all about the benefits of moving our bodies. Remember, this doesn't have to be running three miles. It could be stretching before you go to bed, going to a yoga class, walking to work, or having a ten-minute dance party with your students. Anything that gets your heart pumping and your body moving is a good place to start.

- Start a mediation practice.

Meditation yields surprising benefits. You might want to start by only meditating for a few minutes and then work your way up to a longer practice. I love the Calm app to get started. Journaling is also a form of meditation. This could be a great time to write down your gratitude!

- Wake up fifteen minutes early to enjoy a cup of coffee and quiet time.

The key to this is to put your phone down and be mindful. If you can, sit outside and listen to the birds. Maybe put on your favorite song and sing along. Do something that is going to put you in a good mood for the rest of the day.

- Get creative.

There is no bad way to get creative. Try an adult coloring book, take up painting, or learn to knit. Don't be afraid to think outside the box. Try using sidewalk chalk or taking up pickleball or another fun activity. Play falls in this category. Play is so important to reclaiming our happiness that I have devoted an entire chapter to it. Radical wellness gives us permission to embrace the childlike (not childish) notion of letting go and finding pleasure in the moment.

2. Set aside Time for Radical Wellness

Once you've decided on a radical wellness practice, settle on a regular time for it. Are you going to wake up an fifteen minutes early so you can drink your coffee and settle in for the day? Are you going to pick the kids up from day care thirty minutes after you normally would so you can go for a walk? Is your partner going to tidy up the house three days a week so you have time to paint?

Whatever your radical wellness entails, make sure you have a plan for when and where it's going to take place. Remember this isn't just a fun face mask at the end of the week; this is radical wellness that is crucial to your happiness!

3. Schedule Radical Wellness

You never miss a meeting that you've put on your calendar, and the same should go for taking care of yourself. Do not rely on "I'll see when I can fit radical wellness in." I want you to schedule time for it on your calendar. It's easy to let it fall by the wayside if it isn't scheduled. Remember, this isn't time you have to "earn." You deserve it even when you haven't accomplished as much as you wish.

4. Start Your Practice

Once you've identified the type of radical wellness that you need in your life and the time you can do it, and once you have it on your schedule, the next step is to do it. This might seem obvious, but following through is the hardest part. There is always going to be an excuse not to practice radical wellness. Start with fifteen minutes every day. Be intentional. You can't just hope your practice happens; you need to make it happen.

5. Be Courageous

It's important to recognize that you are the most important person in your life. Seeing that takes courage—the courage to believe in yourself, to love yourself, and to know and feel that you are important.

We know that self-care can be viewed as an add-on. Radical wellness, by contrast, is essential for reversing the mental health crisis in our country—and the plight of teachers today. But thinking beyond self-care to radical wellness requires putting ourselves first, which is not easy given the social constraints that have programmed us to believe that taking care of ourselves is selfish.

Radical wellness requires us to make time for ourselves. This may be done by negotiating new family roles and by saying no to some things in order to say yes to others. But the most important step is changing our mindsets to believe that we are worthy of being taken care of—and that by taking care of ourselves, we are investing in our future, our family's future, and our students' futures. There is so much to say about this that the next three chapters will be an in-depth exploration of specific ways you can start incorporating radical wellness into your life.

Chapter 11

YOU'RE WORTH IT

Recognizing and Cultivating Your Value as an Educator

The teaching profession is full of people with heart. None of us went into education for the so-called summers off, the short hours, or the big paycheck. (I'm joking.) Most of us went into this profession because we care about students and their physical, emotional, and mental well-being. We want our students to get the skills they need to go out into the world, be successful, and contribute in a positive way.

But even with our calling and desire to serve, the reality is that the challenges, demands, and responsibilities of education are escalating. We now feel we are expected to climb an insurmountable mountain only to find ourselves thrown back to the bottom.

This profession can consume our lives, stealing from our waking hours and leaving us feeling like we aren't enough. We toss and turn at night, concerned about the child we placed on the bus yesterday after school who didn't know where he was sleeping because his family was getting evicted from their trailer that day. We are worried about the student who still can't read proficiently after years of being behind, no matter how much extra support we try to give him. We lie there and think about the Coreys in our school who need someone to care for them.

Our emotions are frayed because we deal with behavioral and discipline challenges that are complex and emotionally taxing, and this consumes much of our teachable time. We went to college to become teachers—to teach, influence, and positively impact students' lives. But now our job description has gone from a list of tasks to a full-blown manual that has chapters on counseling, advocating, and caregiving, all on top of teaching. Many times we are expected to serve as teachers, counselors, doctors, parents, mentors, mediators, resource providers, instructional specialists, curriculum specialists, and school leaders. Despite the increased demands, we still don't always have the proper supports we need to be successful.

We feel undervalued by those in society who easily criticize the work we do on behalf of students. An educator's paycheck never matches the value we bring, and while we know why we do what we do, it still gets frustrating. Many teachers start moonlighting because their teacher salary doesn't pay the bills.

It's easy to feel that we aren't valued as education professionals, but I don't want us to be the victims of a system—because that gets us nowhere. Instead, I want to focus on how we can own our value a bit more both in our lives and in our profession.

Finding Our Value

While educators can't change how they are valued by others, they can change how they recognize their own value. A quote from Kate Northrup's book *Money, a Love Story* encapsulates this idea: "If you can't see your value, the world doesn't give you value back."[83] The premise of Northrup's book is that when you don't value yourself, it's difficult to attract abundance of any form in your life, whether it's money, good relationships, reciprocal friendships, love, appreciation, or respect.[84]

When we value ourselves, we believe that we are worthy—of love, happiness, abundance, and all good things. When we genuinely believe we are worthy and that we truly have strength within us, we are more willing to invest in ourselves. When we recognize our inherent worth, we see that spending time, energy, and money on ourselves is a good investment. We also know it's okay to ask for help. If we value ourselves, leaning on support from others makes it easier to take actionable steps toward growth and achieving our goals.

Putting ourselves first because we believe we are worthy is not selfish. The relationship we have with ourselves is the most important relationship in our lives; it is the foundation for every other relationship, as well as our perspective on the world. And a strong relationship with ourselves begins with self-value.

Here's a list of ways we all give away our value. I'm sure we could add more, but I'd like you to place a checkmark down for each one of these that holds true for you.

- ☐ Dismissing compliments
- ☐ Refusing to let others buy you coffee or a meal
- ☐ Making excuses for why you don't need a gift
- ☐ Not asking for help from your partner for chores
- ☐ Not asking your partner for help with the kids
- ☐ Not creating boundaries in your life
- ☐ Letting someone demean you or put you dow
- ☐ Not fighting to get your own needs met
- ☐ Rejecting help from others
- ☐ Sacrificing personal time to grade papers, create lesson plans, etc.

- ☐ Taking on additional responsibilities without any compensation or recognition
- ☐ Allowing your job to become more important than family time
- ☐ Spending your own money on items for the classroom
- ☐ Refusing to choose the restaurant when asked
- ☐ Picking up all the pieces that no one wants to do or because it's expected of you
- ☐ Apologizing for things you shouldn't be sorry for
- ☐ Stopping what you are doing to attend to everyone else's needs
- ☐ Not treating yourself to nice things
- ☐ Refusing to be paid for certain things
- ☐ Constantly giving away advice

- ☐ Nodding instead of speaking
- ☐ Feeling guilt for taking ME time
- ☐ Not protecting your boundaries: checking emails after work hours, etc.
- ☐ Lowering your price or not asking for a raise
- ☐ Not seeking support when facing challenging classroom situations
- ☐ Refusing to ask for help in your classroom
- ☐ Working long hours without proper compensation or overtime pay
- ☐ Providing extra assistance to students without receiving compensation
- ☐ Taking on extra duties, even when you are already overwhelmed
- ☐ Volunteering when you don't have the capacity

It might be shocking to see all the ways we give away our value, but the good news is we can combat this issue by setting boundaries. Given teachers' active investment in their students, and our society's impossible expectations for teachers, it can be hard for educators to set boundaries. The experiences of Amanda, an elementary teacher in my Facebook group, are all too common: "I feel like I constantly need to be available for my students and their families through email or text even when I'm home after school and should be devoting time to my family and my well-being. The school doesn't expect me to do this, but it's something I feel obligated to do. I don't want to let my students or their families down. It's always been my goal for students and families to feel loved and respected, but that goal has somehow turned into a source of anxiety now to be everything for everyone."

This pressure to be available is what so many of us feel as educators. Laura, a second-grade teacher, concurs, writing, "I find myself saying yes to additional leadership roles or committees." Another educator, Ben, feels the crunch of too many commitments. "We lose planning time on a regular basis now due to sub shortages. On other days we lose our time for mandatory trainings that used to happen during release time within the school day. PD now happens during our planning time."

I've done it by saying yes way too many times to things I didn't want to do. For example, I spent the first five years of my business constantly giving my value away. I was hunkered down and in building mode, working sixty to eighty hours a week trying to launch this dream. Miraculously, I started experiencing significant success, and suddenly, my inbox, Facebook messages, text messages, and Instagram messages were full of people who wanted my help. Over and over again, I found myself saying yes to everyone who asked because I cared about them and wanted to be helpful, but all of this was costing me time, energy, and money.

Finally, I had the come-to-Jesus moment where I realized that I needed to start valuing my time and resources more. A lady I didn't know well reached out and asked if we could have lunch because she wanted to pick my brain, as she was considering starting her own business. I agreed, and we spent ninety minutes eating lunch together.

I answered all of her questions, explaining how I'd marketed my business, made connections, created my website, sold my first online course, and launched my first coaching program. I was completely drained by the end of this lunch date, and when she decided it was over, I still hadn't even touched my burger and fries because I had been fielding all of her questions. At the end of the meeting, this woman walked out the door and didn't even offer to pay for lunch.

At first, I was angry at the woman, but then I realized that I was the one who had been offering up my time and expertise to whoever wanted it without realizing how much value I was just giving away. That was on me. Finally, I realized that my time was valuable, which meant I would have to respond differently to the flood of people asking for my advice. I decided that I do like helping and inspiring others, and I certainly want to pour into people, but I needed some hard boundaries going forward.

To avoid these resentments, we need to constantly remember that by valuing ourselves, we live happier lives and equip ourselves to value others. As we set boundaries, we are more capable of respecting boundaries that others set. We can be kind to others and still be kind to ourselves by saying no with grace and humility and by setting boundaries with strength and empathy.

The Joy of Saying No

As I talk with educators, I find that one of the reasons they feel so drained is because they are afraid to draw boundaries in their work life.

How we use our time comes down to simple math. There are only so many hours in a day. We only have so much energy to give. So, it's a simple equation: when we accept one responsibility, something else has to give. For me, the journey of learning to say no has not been easy.

This situation could have been avoided if I had known something that I now tell my coaching clients all the time: every time you say yes to something you don't want to do, you're saying no to the thing you do want to do.

If you say yes to responding to parent emails immediately after your school day, you say no to spending quality, screen-free time with your family. If you say yes to coaching a spring sport, you say no spending your evenings at the gym to improve your health. If you say yes to coming in early to help supervise kids, you say no to getting enough sleep. Every decision we make comes with a sacrifice, and even if it seems like we're doing the right thing by saying yes, those decisions often come back to hurt us.

We do this all the time. We say yes to stuff we don't want to do and then feel resentful, bitter, and ticked, and we act ugly to the people we love because, once again, we've chosen someone or something else over ourselves.

As teachers, we are constantly being asked to help out more, to join this committee or volunteer for that event even if it's not something we want to do. Sometimes it's necessary, but other times we're just getting sucked into too many obligations that take away time we could be spending on making ourselves better teachers. This is where boundaries come into play.

What exactly *is* a boundary? I posed this question to Krista Resnick, who is a boundary expert and master coach. "I don't actually think that there's one flat answer for what a boundary is," she told me. "It depends on where you're at in your boundary journey. For some folks who have run the people-pleasing and maybe codependent pattern for many years, it could be saying no to the things you no longer want to do. It's being honest with yourself and saying, 'This is what I have the capacity for.'"

Teachers are inherently serial people pleasers. We want people to like us. We want to be thought of as "good" people. We believe our worthiness is based on how much we do for others. We are available to everyone. We put others' needs before our own. We do so because we believe we should sacrifice ourselves for others' happiness, we want the approval of others, and generations of teachers before us set the example.

As teachers, our need for approval is a boundary issue, but it's also a self-love issue. Over and over again, we don't put ourselves in the love equation, which affects our ability to create boundaries in our lives and value ourselves.

Not putting yourself at the top of your love equation leaves you feeling depleted, depressed, resentful, and angry. When we aren't our best selves, then we aren't able to give back to the people in our lives who sincerely need us. We must reclaim our rights and start choosing our well-being over making everyone else happy.

How do we start showing ourselves more love? How do we add pleasure, joy, love, laughter, and vitality into our lives? How do we create space in our schedule for the things that light us up rather than diminish our light? An important start is not saying yes to all the stuff we don't want to do. Remember, when we say yes to something we don't want to do, we are saying no to what we do want to do.

How to Know When to Say No

Some of you might be thinking, "Kim, I hear you, but how do I choose what to say no to?" I'm going to guess that most of us should scale back our yeses by about 75 percent, but it's okay if you start out small. Here's a list of questions to help you figure out if you should be saying no to something.

1. Check in with how you feel when you're asked to do a certain thing. Do you feel yucky, angry, ticked already? If so, you should probably say no.

2. Consider if it's something you care deeply about. If so, then it might be worth saying yes even if the work doesn't make you feel good.
3. Does the request conflict with your values, personality, or lifestyle? If baking isn't your thing, it's okay to say no to the bake sale.
4. Is it a good use of your time? Is it contributing to your goals? Sometimes we can do more good for others if we say no and spend that time doing something else.
5. Will it light you up and make you want to keep going? This is the feeling we should all be striving for!

As teachers, we're all used to hearing children say no to things they don't want to do. They're great at setting boundaries, even though it's often frustrating for us adults. Most of us don't remember it, but we were good at setting boundaries once too. But at some point, we lost that ability.

You learned that saying no was impolite, wrong, and inappropriate. You learned to associate no with being dislikable, bad mannered, unkind, or selfish. You didn't want to feel rejected, so you learned to say yes because it made others happy, and you thought that was the most important thing. Saying no was off limits, and yes was the polite and likable thing to say.

However, you are an adult. You are capable of making your own choices, as well as knowing the difference between wrong and right. You know what feels good and doesn't feel good, and you are allowed to honor that part of you. My advice, then, is to start getting comfortable with saying no so you can create more space in your life for the things you want to say yes to!

Declining requests feels uncomfortable, but it's critical to mastering your own health and well-being and harnessing the energy you need to show up as your best self for your class. As teachers, this is going to be difficult at first. Schools work because teachers say yes to way more work than they should. Everyone wants to volunteer for activities that make school special for our students, but at the end of the day, the most important thing we can do for our students is to teach them and love them. If we say yes to all the extra stuff, then we aren't going to be able to come into the classroom with the energy to teach.

One strategy to make saying no easier is to have a script ready. Here's one that I use: "That's so kind and thoughtful to reach out to me about that opportunity. Thank you for thinking of me. As much as I appreciate it, I don't have the capacity to add that to my plate. I hope you can find someone." Or perhaps you can tie it back to your students and also add: "In order to show up for my students this year, I really need the extra time to prepare." When you have a script ready, you feel more confident handling these situations. If you can't remember a script, simply say, "Can you give me some time to think about it?" Then once you get your script ready, you can tell them no. Yes, it takes courage and practice, but we can grow our skillset here and reap the rewards later.

Administrators or other leaders reading this may be freaking out because they're worried about teachers saying no\ to extra duties or requests. This is why we need to do a quick review of the happiness and minimum effective dose (MED) research. Remember, when we are happier, we are more productive. MED research illustrates that the more hours we work over fifty per week, the less we accomplish.[85] Giving people permission to set boundaries and be happier will help create a more dynamic school community. Happiness isn't fluff; it is at the heart of creating a better work environment and better lives—and we all deserve to live our best lives, which is what this book is all about.

When we learn to value ourselves, we learn we are allowed to respect our own feelings and needs. I promise that when you start to own your value, your reserves of well-being will fill up, and you'll feel the reverberation in every area of your life.

Abundance flows to people who value themselves. Good relationships flow to people who value themselves. Good things come to those who value themselves. How is the world, your partner, your school, or the teacher next door supposed to give you value back if you don't own your value? Once you align your inner worth, your outer world will shift—because it always reflects the status of your inner world. I hope that everyone reading this chapter is ready to reclaim their value and start taking back their life.

Chapter 12

THE MAGIC OF PLAY

Unleash the Fun Factor

As a child, I loved to play. I remember spending an entire summer building a treehouse with my brothers and our neighborhood friends amid what felt like a forest to us. We spent hours under a huge maple tree, whacking away at brush and thorns to create our own home, including a living room, kitchen, bedroom, and closets. We packed our lunch each day and sat under the big maple tree in our treehouse kitchen with our table made from logs and wood slats, enjoying our bologna and cheese sandwiches and chips. We felt like we were big stuff. We delighted in creating and playing. Even now, I remember this time as magical. I still run into my childhood friend Derek, who has the same nostalgic feelings that I do about our treehouse.

As children, play comes effortlessly and naturally to us. We find what brings us joy and do it. But as we grow older, engaging in play becomes frivolous and silly to us, maybe even a waste of time; for now, we must be grown-ups. Or we think, "Who in the heck has time for play? Have you seen what I do for a living, sister?"

Not only has play been stripped out of our adult lives, but it's even being stripped out of our students' lives. When I started teaching, our kindergarten rooms had kitchens and stoves because kids learned to cook, experiment, and create. But I'll never forget when one of my superintendents came in and decided we had to remove the play kitchens because we had to focus on teaching our students reading and writing. No more lollygagging around with all that play.

I also remember having three recesses a day with my students: one midmorning, one after lunch, and a short one in the afternoon. Eventually, our school had to go down to only an after-lunch recess. Unfortunately, some schools have adopted a no-recess policy because of the harsh consequences and fear-driven mandates from state policymakers regarding scores and academics.

Play is just not what it used to be. In fact, a Michigan State University study found that children today spend 50 percent less time outside than children did twenty years ago.[86] Outdoor play has been replaced with an average of six and a half hours a day on electronic media.[87] Sadly, the expression "Let's go out and play" is a phrase of the past.

As teachers, we know our students need more time to play, create, and nurture a sense of wonder and curiosity, but we are trapped in an education system driven by test results. Even though the research shows that free time and unstructured play are essential for intellectual and emotional growth, socialization, and cooperation, test scores and hard-core academics still win out.

Although we know play is important for our students, we rarely think about how play is also essential for our continued development as educators. Research promotes the idea that while we don't have to play all the time, a little bit of play goes a long way toward making us happier and more productive. Scientists have found that play is important to the development of brains in both humans and other species. Animal play has evolved over eons to promote survival, making animals smarter and more adaptable. For more intelligent species, play enhances empathy. For humans, play sparks creativity and innovation.[88] In this way, play is a fundamental component of success.

In *Play: How It Shapes the Brain, Opens the Imagination, and Invigorates the Soul*, Dr. Stuart Brown explains that play is important in making us smarter, more creative, and better at solving problems.[89] Play comes in many forms, whether it's attending a painting class on a Sunday afternoon, learning to play a new sport, or dancing to "Don't Stop Believin'" in your living room. Regardless of the shape it takes, play not only improves mood but also increases productivity and builds stronger relationships. As Stuart Brown explains, play is anything but trivial; he goes so far as to say that play is "a biological drive as integral to our health as sleep or nutrition . . . The power of play is intensely pleasurable. It energizes us and enlivens us. It eases our burdens. It renews our natural sense of optimism and opens us up to new possibilities."[90]

The "intensely pleasurable" nature of play has transformed my clients' lives. I was coaching a client who had three young children and a very demanding job as a hospital administrator. She felt depressed and lost in her life and wondered if this was just how it was supposed to be as a mom and a full-time career woman. We started to discuss things that she used to love before she became a mother, wife, and career woman. She began to cry and said, "Kim, I used to love to listen to music. I haven't listened to music that I love for over ten years. How did this happen?" This woman was so caught up in all of her roles that she had simply forgotten that music brings her joy.

Returning to Play

It's so easy to lose ourselves and who we once were. But we are allowed to hold on to pieces of ourselves before we become everything to everyone. When we live a life that feels expansive and has moments of fun and bliss, it means we are participating in something greater than ourselves. We are just in the pure joy of the moment.

While it has childish associations, play can benefit educators of all ages. How, then, can we re-center the role of play in our lives?

Reincorporating play as a daily habit is a lot easier once we understand the kinds of play that most benefit us. Dr. Brown spent years observing people and found that most have a dominant mode of play that falls into one of eight "play personalities."[91] I go over these below and give you some examples. Most of us have a mix of these personalities, so circle all the categories that resonate with you and make you feel happy.

The Joker: This person likes to goof around, play practical jokes, and engage in nonsense. My family is full of this personality. We participate in constant pranking. It might be my husband sending my mom a fake bill in the mail showing she owes $8,000 in back taxes, or it could be me pranking my brother with a fake call from his son's school proclaiming his son got in a fight, or it might be my brother making up a story to get me all riled up. This joking goes on and on and we still fall for it.

The Kinesthetic: These are people who like to move. Yes, that movement can be athletic, but it can also include dancing, swimming, yoga, or walking. Some people naturally want to push their bodies and feel the result. They need to be in motion to think. I would say this is another category I fall into. I feel most alive when I'm moving my body. I might play pickleball with my husband and son, take a run, or play hide-and-seek each night with my dogs while my husband goes to the gym. (He purposely leaves for the gym during my playtime with the dogs because he says it gets on his nerves.)[92]

The Explorer: People with this play personality yearn for either physical or mental exploration, like going to new places, hearing new music, researching new subjects, and discovering new experiences. They're motivated by a sense of uncovering new things and finding the unexpected. Exploration can be physical, mental, or emotional, but it must be about finding the new. Think Steve Irwin, Jane Goodall, and Bear Grylls from the show *Man vs. Wild*.[93]

The Competitor: Competitors feel alive while playing competitive games with specific rules, and they play to win! They are all about keeping score and fighting to be number one. Competition might involve chess, video games, team sports, or solitary challenges. I'm afraid I fall into this one too; I am a scorekeeper for almost everything in my life.[94]

The Director: These people love planning and executing activities and social events; they are born organizers. They love to throw a party and are the instigators of vacation plans. These are the people who love to research, make reservations early, and put together special goodie bags for everyone on the trip. For directors, organizing the event or the trip and making sure everything goes smoothly is just as fun as the thing itself.[95]

The Collector: Collectors enjoy collecting and categorizing things (coins, trains, antiques) and ticking stuff off their bucket list. They love the thrill of getting the best and most interesting collection of objects or experiences. Our friends David and Jane are collectors. They love going to auctions and finding antiques and old pieces of furniture to redo. Their entire basement is full of Coca-Cola memorabilia. They get excited to tell us about their new findings, and they even have an entire shed devoted to their hobby.[96]

The Artist/Creator: People with these play personalities enjoy making things. Their creativity might involve restoring an old truck, decorating a room, enjoying arts and crafts, cooking, painting, woodworking, gardening, sewing, scrapbooking, etc. My friend Jamila worked as an anthropologist and then as a nutrition coach before she followed her joy by devoting herself to art and painting, which had been her childhood dream. She immersed herself in her play personality and now has a full-time business where she creates paintings of beautiful bouquets and rambling landscapes, shipping them around the world to buyers. You never know what following your play might lead you to.[97]

The Storyteller: This person loves to be immersed in their imagination. They might like writing, reading novels, playwriting, acting, learning magic tricks, watching movies, or screenwriting. They like to experience the thoughts and emotions of the characters in a story. My editor Zosha falls into this category. She has been a writer her whole life, and from a young age she loved coming up with stories. Being able to use her words to dream up new characters, situations, and emotions is how she plays. She recently shared that she's writing a comedy pilot, so maybe she's a bit of a joker too.[98]

Steps for Incorporating Play

Once you've identified your play personalities, it's time to reflect on how best to bring play back into your life.

1. Think about what you did as a child that got you excited or brought you joy. Was it arts and crafts at school? Helping Dad fix the lawnmower or build things? Did you like group play or solitary play?
2. Jot down the play personalities that most resonated with you. What opportunities within each play personality might energize you? What do you see yourself enjoying?
3. Find opportunities to play more in your life. How can you be more open to play both in your classroom and your personal life?
4. Give yourself permission to be playful and have fun and just see what happens.

For teachers, incorporating play might look like having a dance party at the start of class each morning or joining a group of students who are playing hopscotch. It's easy to find ways to play at school because we see our students do it all day. But even more importantly, this is about playing outside of the classroom. It's about remembering what brings you joy, makes you laugh, inspires you, and makes you feel good. Look at the list you made based on the questions above and ensure you're finding time for the joy of play.

If you're a school leader, how might you incorporate more play into the workplace? I know of an elementary principal who ditched the Friday morning faculty meeting and replaced it with Fun Fridays, where the entire staff engages in a game or other activity. It might be a dodgeball match, a silly group project, or a game inspired by *Minute to Win It*.

The principal said it has changed the climate of the school and done wonders for the teachers, especially after an exhausting week. Teachers love it so much that they race to this principal's office each Friday and ask if they can plan the next Fun Friday. Another school participates in what they call Joy Clubs, where they come together once every two weeks to participate in some type of fun activity.

Fun is your North Star, and it's in your nature to desire it. It's time we give ourselves permission to play and be playful. It's time to bring back that inner child who loved to bask in the rain, inhale the scent of flowers, or frolic in the field with their dog. When we play, all areas of our lives tend to improve. We begin to feel alive and aligned with our spirits. We begin to feel true exhilaration simply in living life right here at this moment. It's time to follow your bliss.

Play is about changing patterns and activities in our lives, but it also is about an attitude of playfulness. We can learn to bring more excitement and adventure into our lives and make work an extension of our play so we can feel engaged and happy.

Chapter 13
THE RIPPLE OF HOPE

Embracing Small Changes for Big Impact

I always loved asking students, neighbors, and my son's friends one question: "Who's the best teacher you ever had?" The follow-up question was the critical part: "Why?" Over and over again, I always got a version of the same two answers.

"My teacher was happy." Or "My teacher cared about me."

The best thing we can do for our students is to take care of our teachers.

I've given you many strategies in this book for increasing your happiness set point, and I've described the scientific evidence that supports those techniques. I know this might feel overwhelming or even intimidating. It's unrealistic to incorporate all of these strategies into your life at once or to do them all of the time. Instead, focus on making small changes in your life that will build upon each other and end up having a huge impact.

To think about the cumulative effect of those small changes, I want to talk about compound interest. As we know, compound interest is the interest we earn from the original amount (or principal) of an investment plus any interest we've already made through that investment. When we invest with compound interest, we earn interest on top of interest. Compound interest is the secret sauce for building wealth, and it's one of the most basic principles of investing. But what does it have to do with happiness?

Many times, people think they have to take massive action to change their lives, but in reality, small changes over time can make a big difference, just like when we invest with compound interest. We may not even realize we're making progress, but tiny adjustments build toward a snowball effect that works.

Author James Clear writes about this same principle in his book, *Atomic Habits*, which goes in depth about how making small changes in our day is the key to making big improvements in our lives. He writes that "improving by 1% isn't particularly notable—sometimes it isn't even noticeable—but it can be far more meaningful, especially in the long run."[99]

When you're first starting, writing down what you're grateful for before leaving for work might not make a big difference; in fact, it might not even improve your morning. But the next morning you might realize it's a bit easier to come up with three things you're grateful for, and that could improve your day. When you start your day off in a good mood, you might be calmer and better able to handle difficult situations in the classroom. When you get home, instead of being exhausted from a stressful day, you might have more energy to take a walk or go to a workout class. These small habits have a powerful ripple effect.

This book is not a magic pill; it's a blueprint for action. It's not enough to just read it—you have to decide to make the moves in your life to improve your emotional health.

We can't do it all. But what if you just select one or two strategies that *might* work for you? There's a reason you picked up this book and chose to read it. You deserve to take your power back, starting right now, so you can begin to drive your life in a direction that is meaningful and purposeful to you. Remember to focus on how you want to feel in your life and then pursue the thoughts, actions, and behaviors that lead you toward those feelings.

This book puts the power in your hands—you and only you have the power to change your life. But you must begin doing things differently to get a different outcome. You deserve a version of yourself that is moving toward getting happier. I want to tell you that you can make this happen. But while I know these tools work, I also know it's really easy to fall back into our old programming. Uncomfortable doesn't feel good. Hard doesn't feel good.

I recently saw the following quote from mental health professional Dr. Vassilia Binensztok:

> When you're not used to being confident, Confidence feels like arrogance.
>
> When you're used to being passive, Assertiveness feels like aggression.
>
> When you're not used to getting your needs met, Prioritizing yourself feels selfish.
>
> Your comfort zone is not a good benchmark.[100]

We don't grow by staying in our comfort zones. We must become creatures of discomfort. The real work has to be done from the deep recesses of our soul.

I am reminded of the kits I received as a fourth-grade teacher during a unit on the life cycle of butterflies. I set up the pop-up habitat for the butterflies, and my classroom watched the progress each day. First, each caterpillar formed a chrysalis, and then each underwent a tremendous change. The caterpillar releases digestive juices that break down most of its body into a "tissue cell soup" from which it develops four wings, new legs, new eyes, new mouthparts, and genitalia. It was a grueling process to watch.

My students and I would monitor the cocoons every day, hoping to see some type of life. We began to observe just tiny movements, and it was painstaking to watch because the butterflies were hardly making any progress. They would struggle and struggle as if there were no end to their development. I remember thinking that I just wanted to use a paperclip and make a small slit in the cocoons to help free them. But doing this would stunt the butterflies' wing development, and because of that they would never be able to reach their full potential and fly.

You see, the butterfly has to have a productive struggle. It has to go through the process of fighting its way out, and by doing so, its wings fill with blood, and it is born strong. And as the familiar metaphor goes, if a caterpillar chose to stay a caterpillar—if she decided the chaos of metamorphosis was too much—she would never know what she could become.

I know all too well how hard the struggle is, and it can feel easier to choose comfort, but over and over again, life has proved to me that on the other side of comfort is greatness.

I wrote this book because I wanted to help teachers find the greatness they deserve. I don't want you to keep doing the same thing over and over and expecting a different result. In that light, I recently learned a concept from a friend that I think makes a fitting conclusion to this project. The Zulu tribe in Africa have a greeting, *sawubona*, that translates to "I see you, you are important to me, and I value you." Sawubona carries the importance of recognizing the worth and dignity of each person. It says, "I see the whole of you—your experiences, your passions, your pain, your strengths and weaknesses, and your future. You are valuable to me." Sawubona is also infused with the belief that when others "see" us, we exist.

I want you to know, friend, that I do see you. I see what you are doing day in and day out on behalf of your students. I see your anguished faces and your exhaustion. I know you aren't always valued for the grand job that is bestowed upon you. It's so easy to feel discounted, undervalued, and underappreciated, so while we certainly believe that every student matters, I also want to say every teacher matters too. You count too. I *see* you.

This profession is all about the heart. You are the one who said yes to teaching and leading, yes to mentoring, yes to influencing, and yes to changing lives. You made a commitment not only to yourself but also to the world—a commitment to show up fully and completely with grace and enthusiasm as a leader for kids when you are needed most.

But you did not make the commitment to lose everything else that is important to you: yourself, your family, your hobbies, and your well-being.

Most importantly, I want you to know that you count too. Your well-being matters too. Your peace matters too. Your family matters too. Your mental health matters too. You are allowed to have a life outside this profession. I hope you have the courage to reclaim the other parts of yourself that are just as important as teaching students. Sawubona, my friend. I am rooting for you in all ways.

BIBLIOGRAPHY

Achor, Shawn. *The Happiness Advantage*. New York: Crown Publishers, 2010.

Achor, Shawn. "The Happy Secret to Better Work." Filmed May 2011 in Bloomington, IN. TED video, 12:15. https://www.ted.com/talks/shawn_achor_the_happy_secret_to_better_work?language=en.

Aknin, Lara B., et al. "Prosocial Spending and Well-Being: Cross-Cultural Evidence for a Psychological Universal." Working paper, National Bureau of Economic Research, September 2010.

Baraz, James and Shoshana Alexander. "The Helper's High." *Greater Good Magazine*, February 1, 2010. https://greatergood.berkeley.edu/article/item/the_helpers_high.

Bieber, Christy. "Revealing Divorce Statistics in 2024." *Forbes*, January 8, 2024. https://www.forbes.com/advisor/legal/divorce/divorce-statistics/.

Bloom, Paul. "What Becoming a Parent Really Does to Your Happiness." *The Atlantic*, November 2, 2021. https://www.theatlantic.com/family/archive/2021/11/does-having-kids-make-you-happy/620576/.

Brown, Brené. *The Gifts of Imperfection*. Center City, MN: Hazelden, 2010.

Brown, Brené with Dr. Susan David. "On the Dangers of Toxic Positivity (Part 1 of 2)." *Unlocking Us with Brené Brown*, March 1, 2021. Podcast, 1:05:41. https://brenebrown.com/podcast/brene-with-dr-susan-david-on-the-dangers-of-toxic-positivity-part-1-of-2/.

Brooks, Arthur C. *Build the Life You Want: The Art and Science of Getting Happier*. New York: Penguin Press, 2023.

Carter, Christine. *Raising Happiness: 10 Simple Steps for More Joyful Kids and Happier Parents*. New York: Random House, 2010.

Csikszentmihalyi, Mihaly. *Flow: The Psychology of Optimal Experience*. New York: Harper & Row, 1990.

Clear, James. *Atomic Habits: An Easy & Proven Way to Build Good Habits & Break Bad Ones*. New York: Avery, 2018.

Clear, James. "How to Build New Habits: This Is Your Strategy Guide." Website of James Clear. https://jamesclear.com/new-habit.

Diener, Ed and Robert Biswas-Diener. "Will Money Increase Subjective Well-Being?: A Literature Review and Guide to Needed Research." *Social Indicators Research* 57, no. 2 (2002): 119–69. http://www.jstor.org/stable/27526987.

Diener, Ed, and Martin E.P. Seligman. "Very Happy People." *Psychological Science* 13, no. 1 (January 2002).

Dyer, Wayne. "The Power of I Am." *Wayne's Blog*. Website of Wayne Dyer. https://www.drwaynedyer.com/blog/the-power-of-i-am/#:~:text=Then%20make%20the%20shift%20in,define%20your%20concept%20of%20yourself.

Education Support. "Teacher Wellbeing Index 2019." London: Education Support, 2019. https://www.educationsupport.org.uk/media/b1qbtmzl/teacher_wellbeing_index_2019.pdf.

Escalante, Alison. "New Science on Stress: Feeling Your Feelings Works Better Than Toughing It Out." *Forbes*, October 20, 2020. https://www.forbes.com/sites/alisonescalante/2020/10/20/new-science-on-stress-feeling-your-feelings-works-better-than-toughing-it-out/?sh=2c1e6d40516a.

Ferriss, Timothy. *The 4-Hour Workweek*. New York: Crown Publishing Group, 2007.

Frankl, Viktor E. *Man's Search for Meaning*. Boston: Beacon Press, 2006.

Ganssle, Jack. "The Rule of Fifty." The Ganssle Group, March 10, 2008. http://www.ganssle.com/rants/theruleoffifty.htm.

Harvard Health Publishing. "Giving Thanks Can Make You Happier." *Harvard Health Publishing*, August 14, 2021. https://www.health.harvard.edu/healthbeat/giving-thanks-can-make-you-happier.

Healthy Brains. "Brain Facts." Website of Healthy Brains. https://healthybrains.org/brain-facts/.

Hintzen, Katy. "The Consequences of Children Spending Less Time Outdoors." Michigan State University Extension, July 2, 2015. https://www.canr.msu.edu/news/the_consequences_of_children_spending_less_time_outdoors.

Klein, Alyson. "1,500 Decisions a Day (at Least!): How Teachers Cope with a Dizzying Array of Questions." Education Week, December 6, 2021. https://www.edweek.org/teaching-learning/1-500-decisions-a-day-at-least-how-teachers-cope-with-a-dizzying-array-of-questions/2021/12.

Malcolm, Sarah. *Forbes*. "To Increase Productivity, Work Less and Get Happy." https://www.forbes.com/sites/forbesagencycouncil/2021/04/16/if-you-want-to-be-more-productive-at-work-get-happy/?sh=4d9723017be2y/.

ENDNOTES

1. Sonja Lyubomirsky, *The How of Happiness* (New York: Penguin Books, 2008), 72.
2. "What Is Positive Psychology?" Positive Psychology Institute, accessed May 25, 2023, https://positivepsychologyinstitute.com.au/what-is-positive-psychology.
3. Shawn Achor, *The Happiness Advantage* (New York: Crown Publishers, 2010), 10.
4. Shawn Achor, "The Happy Secret to Better Work," filmed May 2011, TED video, 12:15, https://www.ted.com/talks/shawn_achor_the_happy_secret_to_better_work?language=en.
5. Arthur C. Brooks, *Build the Life You Want* (New York: Penguin Press, 2023), 5.
6. Brooks, *Build the Life*, 5.
7. Brooks, *Build the Life*, 5–6.
8. Lyubomirsky, *How of Happiness*, 21.
9. Lyubomirsky, *How of Happiness*, 51.
10. Viktor E. Frankl, *Man's Search for Meaning* (Boston: Beacon Press, 2006).
11. Frankl, *Search for Meaning*, 17.
12. Lyubomirsky, *How of Happiness*, 28.
13. Lyubomirsky, *How of Happiness*, 29.
14. Lyubomirsky, *How of Happiness*, 30.
15. Ed Diener and Robert Biswas-Diener, "Will Money Increase Subjective Well-Being?: A Literature Review and Guide to Needed Research," *Social Indicators Research* 57, no. 2 (2002): 119–69, http://www.jstor.org/stable/27526987.
16. Lyubomirsky, *How of Happiness*, 65.
17. Lyubomirsky, *How of Happiness*, 64–65.
18. Paul Bloom, "What Becoming a Parent Really Does to Your Happiness," *The Atlantic*, November 2, 2021, https://www.theatlantic.com/family/archive/2021/11/does-having-kids-make-you-happy/620576/.
19. S. K. Nelson, K. Kushlev, and S. Lyubomirsky, "The Pains and Pleasures of Parenting: When, Why, and How Is Parenthood Associated with More or Less Well-Being?" (unpublished manuscript, 2014), University of California, Riverside, https://sonjalyubomirsky.com/files/2012/09/Nelson-Kushlev-Lyubomirsky-in-press1.pdf.

20	Nelson, Kushlev, and Lyubomirsky, "Pains and Pleasures of Parenting."
21	Brené Brown with Dr. Susan David, "On the Dangers of Toxic Positivity (Part 1 of 2)," March 1, 2021, *Unlocking Us with Brene Brown*, podcast, 1:05:41, https://brenebrown.com/podcast/brene-with-dr-susan-david-on-the-dangers-of-toxic-positivity-part-1-of-2/.
22	Brown, "Dangers of Toxic Positivity."
23	Brown, "Dangers of Toxic Positivity."
24	Brown, "Dangers of Toxic Positivity."
25	Alison Escalante, "New Science on Stress: Feeling Your Feelings Works Better Than Toughing It Out," *Forbes*, October 20, 2020, https://www.forbes.com/sites/alisonescalante/2020/10/20/new-science-on-stress-feeling-your-feelings-works-better-than-toughing-it-out/?sh=2e7a419d516a.
26	Achor, "Happy Secret."
27	Achor, "Happy Secret."
28	Achor, "Happy Secret."
29	Achor, "The Happy Secret."
30	Alyson Klein, "1,500 Decisions a Day (at Least!): How Teachers Cope with a Dizzying Array of Questions," Education Week, December 6, 2021, https://www.edweek.org/teaching-learning/1-500-decisions-a-day-at-least-how-teachers-cope-with-a-dizzying-array-of-questions/2021/12.
31	Shawn Achor, "To Increase Productivity, Work Less and Get Happy," website of Shawn Achor, https://www.shawnachor.com/project/huffington-post-to-increase-productivity-work-less-get-happy/.
32	Achor, "Happy Secret."
33	Achor, "Happy Secret."
34	Dan Pink, *A Whole New Mind* (New York: Riverhead Books, 2006), 85.
35	"Teacher Wellbeing Index 2019," Education Support, 2019, https://www.educationsupport.org.uk/media/b1qbtmzl/teacher_wellbeing_index_2019.pdf.
36	"Teacher Wellbeing."
37	Mihaly Csikszentmihalyi, *Flow: The Psychology of Optimal Experience* (New York: Harper & Row, 1990), page not provided.
38	Jeremy Sutton, "Wheel of Life Coaching," Positive Psychology, July 29, 2020, https://positivepsychology.com/wheel-of-life-coaching/.
39	"Giving Thanks Can Make You Happier," *Harvard Health Publishing*, August 14, 2021, https://www.health.harvard.edu/healthbeat/giving-thanks-can-make-you-happier.
40	"Brain Facts," Healthy Brains, https://healthybrains.org/brain-facts/.
41	Charlotte Johnson, "Stuck on Negative Thinking," Care Counseling, https://care-clinics.com/stuck-on-negative-thinking/#:~:text=According%20to%20the%20National%20Science,—relationships%2C%20work%2C%20school.

42 Johnson, "Stuck on Negative Thinking."
43 Motohide Miyahara, et al., "Functional Connectivity Between Amygdala and Facial Regions Involved in Recognition of Facial Threat," *Social Cognitive and Affective Neuroscience* 8, no. 2 (February 2013): 181–189, https://doi.org/10.1093/scan/nsr085.
44 Achor, "Happy Secret."
45 Wayne Dyer, "The Power of I Am," *Wayne's Blog*, https://www.drwaynedyer.com/blog/the-power-of-i-am/#:~:text=Then%20make%20the%20shift%20in,define%20your%20concept%20of%20yourself.
46 James Clear, *Atomic Habits: An Easy & Proven Way to Build Good Habits & Break Bad Ones* (New York: Avery, 2018), 29.
47 James Clear, "How to Build New Habits: This is Your Strategy Guide," website of James Clear, https://jamesclear.com/new-habit.
48 *Stutz*, directed by Jonah Hill, released November 14, 2022, distributed by Netflix.
49 *Stutz*.
50 *Stutz*.
51 Achor, "Happy Secret."
52 Lyubomirsky, *How of Happiness*, 23.
53 Lyubomirsky, *How of Happiness*, 244–247.
54 Lisa Mosconi, *The XX Brain* (New York: Avery, 2020), 227.
55 Mosconi, *XX Brain*, 226.
56 Mosconi, *XX Brain*, 225.
57 Brené Brown, *The Gifts of Imperfection* (Center City, MN: Hazelden, 2010), 19.
58 Brown, *Gifts of Imperfection*, 19.
59 *Stutz*.
60 Lyubomirsky, *How of Happiness*, 125.
61 Epicurus, *The Essential Epicurus* (Buffalo, NY: Prometheus Books, 1993).
62 Ed Diener and Martin E.P. Seligman, "Very Happy People," *Psychological Science* 13, no. 1 (January 2002): page not provided.
63 Lyubomirsky, *How of Happiness*, 138.
64 Lyubomirsky, *How of Happiness*, 139–140.
65 Lyubomirsky, *How of Happiness*, 138.
66 Zara Abrams, "Science of Friendship," *American Psychological Association Monitor on Psychology* 54, no. 4 (June 1, 2023): page not provided, https://www.apa.org/monitor/2023/06/cover-story-science-friendship.
67 Lyubomirsky, *How of Happiness*, 140.
68 "The Surgeon General's Advisory on the Importance of Social Connection for Health and Well-Being," U.S. Department of Health and Human Services, Surgeon General's advisory, (2023), https://www.

    hhs.gov/sites/default/files/surgeon-general-social-connection-advisory.pdf.
69 Lyubomirsky, *How of Happiness*, 139.
70 Christy Bieber, "Revealing Divorce Statistics in 2024," *Forbes*, January 8, 2024, https://www.forbes.com/advisor/legal/divorce/divorce-statistics/.
71 Lyubomirsky, *How of Happiness*, 141.
72 Lyubomirsky, *How of Happiness*, 141–142.
73 Lara B. Aknin, et al. "Prosocial Spending and Well-Being: Cross-Cultural Evidence for a Psychological Universal" (working paper), September 2010).
74 Christine Carter, *Raising Happiness: 10 Simple Steps for More Joyful Kids and Happier Parents* (New York: Random House, 2010), page not provided.
75 Natalie Angier, "The Biology Behind the Milk of Human Kindness," *The New York Times*, November 23, 2009, https://www.nytimes.com/2009/11/24/science/24angier.html?_r=1&partner=rss&emc=rss.
76 James Baraz and Shoshana Alexander, "The Helper's High," *Greater Good Magazine*, February 1, 2010, https://greatergood.berkeley.edu/article/item/the_helpers_high.
77 Jack Ganssle, "The Rule of Fifty," The Ganssle Group, March 10, 2008, http://www.ganssle.com/rants/theruleoffifty.htm.
78 Achor, "Happy Secret."
79 Timothy Ferriss, *The 4-Hour Workweek* (New York: Crown Publishing Group, 2007).
80 "WHO Highlights Urgent Need to Transform Mental Health and Mental Health Care," World Health Organization, June 17, 2022, https://www.who.int/news/item/17-06-2022-who-highlights-urgent-need-to-transform-mental-health-and-mental-health-care#:~:text=Social%20and%20economic%20inequalities%2C%20public,year%20of%20the%20pandemic%20alone.
81 Eve Rodsky, *Fair Play* (New York: G. P. Putnam's Sons, 2019), 10–11.
82 Daniella Silva, "'We're Human, Too': Simone Biles Highlights Importance of Mental Health," NBC News, July 27, 2021, https://www.nbcnews.com/news/olympics/we-re-human-too-simone-biles-highlights-importance-mental-health-n1275224.
83 Kate Northrup, *Money, a Love Story* (Carlsbad, CA: Hay House, 2013), 45.
84 Northrup, *Money*, 46–49.
85 Ganssle, "Rule of Fifty."
86 Katy Hintzen, "The Consequences of Children Spending Less Time Outdoors," Michigan State University

	Extension, July 2, 2015, https://www.canr.msu.edu/news/the_consequences_of_children_spending_less_time_outdoors.
87	Hintzen, "Less Time Outdoors."
88	Stuart Brown and Christopher Vaughan, *Play: How It Shapes the Brain, Opens the Imagination, and Invigorates the Soul* (New York: Avery, 2009), 5.
89	Brown and Vaughan, *Play*, page not provided.
90	Brown and Vaughan, *Play*, 5.
91	Brown and Vaughan, *Play*, 65.
92	Brown and Vaughan, *Play*, 66–67.
93	Brown, Vaughan, *Play*, 67.
94	Brown, Vaughan, *Play*, 67–68.
95	Brown, Vaughan, *Play*, 68.
96	Brown, Vaughan, *Play*, 69.
97	Brown, Vaughan, *Play*, 69.
98	Brown, Vaughan, *Play*, 69.
99	Clear, *Atomic Habits*, 15.
100	Dr. Vassilia (@DrVassilia), "When you're not used to being confident, confidence feels like arrogance, X, May 23, 2021, 9:52 a.m., https://twitter.com/DrVassilia/status/1234567890123456789.

ACKNOWLEDGMENTS

Writing this book has definitely been a team effort. About once a year for ten years, I would tell my husband, Scott, "I'm going to write that book." Each time, he believed that I would. He never lost faith in me and has continued to support me and my dream of empowering educators. He greets me with flowers when I've had tough travel weeks and never hesitates to tell me how proud he is of me. His solid support throughout this whole entrepreneurial journey gives me the firm foundation from which to spread my wings and fly. He truly is one of the good guys.

I'm forever grateful for Matthew Kanneberg and his wife, Karin, who lent me their golden nugget of paradise, their vacation home in Lake Elmore, Vermont. It was 2020, and I was struggling with getting chapters written for my book (once again) even though I felt I had the words and stories inside of me. I made a post on Facebook asking if anyone could recommend a quiet place where I might go by myself to zero in on my book. Matthew, a high school classmate and friend of our family, sent me a message and offered up his mountain retreat. In the fall of 2020, I spent two and a half weeks with just my dog, Sophie, for companionship, writing, reflecting, hiking, and soul-searching. Sophie and I spent early mornings hiking Elmore Mountain, and then I spent the afternoons and evenings sitting on the back porch of the beautiful cottage writing many of the words you find in this book. The inspiration from nature all around me gave me the peace I needed to reach into the recesses of my soul and write these words. There was even a pond that looked like Henry David Thoreau's Walden Pond. My surroundings provided great peace, solitude, and reflection, which brought some of my writing to fruition.

When I agreed to write this book for IMPress, I still feared that I lacked the adequate skills. I'm more of a visionary—someone who can see where they want to go in the future and orally tell meaningful stories. I didn't believe in myself as a writer. I'm also not someone who will reread something seventeen times to make sure it's organized the right way or that it's a good enough rough draft to submit. One day it came to me that my previous superintendent and friend, Mary Roberson, was an excellent writer who had started her own consulting business, Bower Consulting (BowerConsult.com). I proposed hiring her as my editor and she agreed. Not only that but her daughter Zosha (of ZoshaMarie.com) was just graduating with her MFA in creative writing, so they decided to tag team it. What a gift they have been to me in getting this book out into the world.

And of course, thanks to IMPress and the Reading List and their entire editing team, who also brought all the magic touches to make this book beautiful and easy to read.

ABOUT THE AUTHOR

Kim Strobel is an internationally known motivational speaker for schools, businesses, and organizations, and she travels the globe sharing the impact of happiness and its connection to success.

Kim is a powerhouse influencer, consultant, and happiness coach whose work shapes the way schools, businesses, and organizations reclaim their happiness, ignite their passion, and lead with purpose. Her "real talk" attitude is a refreshing approach that allows her to authentically connect with audiences everywhere.

During her twenty-five-year education career, she has partnered with people at all levels to implement innovative and inspirational practices in the classroom, increase academic achievement, and create positive school-wide climates.

Companies like Google as well as state departments of education, schools, and organizations call on Kim to help them prioritize their health and well-being so they can live a life that feels good from the inside out.

While Kim loves inspiring others, her most important job has been being a momma to her son, Spencer, a wife to her husband, Scott, and of course a dog momma to her three rescue dogs, George, Sophie, and Luna. She's also a stepmom to Drew, Sidney, and Clair, a devoted runner and lover of books, and she has had a Friday lunch date with her beloved one-hundred-year-old grandmother for twenty-three years. Another passion of Kim's is rescuing dogs who have been abandoned or mistreated—to date, she has rescued or rehomed 208 dogs. A portion of her book sales will fund her animal rescue missions, Happy Tails Inc. and Rivers Edge Animal Shelter. Kim resides in Tell City, Indiana. Her website is www.strobeleducation.com.

SPEAKING TOPICS

The Science of Happiness: Ignite Your Spark & Unleash Your Potential

When you hear the terms *happiness* and *well-being*, what do you think of? In this keynote, Kim uses storytelling and science to talk about how happiness is more than just a feeling—in fact, it can have a tremendous effect on performance.

Happy employees are 31 percent more productive, ten times more engaged in their jobs, and three times more creative. Learning the happiness success formula is a paradigm shift in how we navigate our work lives and our personal lives.

With an energy that's both captivating and down-to-earth, Kim shares eye-opening research and simple, actionable steps for how we can reprogram our brains to become more fulfilled and positive in our personal and professional lives.

Remember Your Why: How to Reclaim Your Purpose and Ignite Your Passion

As we navigate the heavy toll that the pandemic has taken on both student progress and teacher morale, it's time to give teachers a reason to find joy and purpose in their profession again.

In this keynote, Kim recalls her experiences as a classroom teacher, sharing a heartfelt story that gives new meaning to being an educator. Her open and honest approach will make your staff feel affirmed and rejuvenated as she acknowledges the real-life challenges teachers are facing right now and provides a fresh perspective for the school year ahead. You will leave feeling more connected to your calling, and you'll gain the energy to teach with purpose!

Radical Wellness: The Self-Care Nobody's Talking About

Self-care is an overused term that doesn't get to the heart of what educators are facing each day. They are told to practice self-care when they're already drowning in a sea of mental and physical fatigue. It's time to replace *self-care* with *radical wellness*.

It's radical because it's uncomfortable and messy, and it requires us to examine our lives from the inside out, including taking a step back and making some much-needed moves. It is not a random, long-overdue pampering with a facial or a walk in the park. Kim shares real tools that teach you how to prioritize yourself in a way that shifts your thinking. It's about moving beyond self-care to create a new outlook on life that is empowering and transformative—putting ourselves first so that we can live happier lives for ourselves and others.

The Science of Growth Mindset: Change Your Thoughts to Increase Your Success

In this keynote, Kim shares how cultivating a growth mindset can shift the way we think about our current circumstances so we can embrace challenges and obstacles as a means to growth.

Mindsets are a set of beliefs that affect how we think about our abilities, how we behave, and the actions we take toward our goals. When we take intentional steps to prioritize a growth mindset in the workplace, we impact the school culture and help build growth mindset habits that fuel educators' success.

Your audience will walk away with tools to evaluate their beliefs so that they can face obstacles with a more productive approach, learning and developing new skills in the process with a focus on improvement.

MORE FROM IMPRESS

Empower: What Happens when Students Own Their Learning by A.J. Juliani and John Spencer

Learner-Centered Innovation: Spark Curiosity, Ignite Passion, and Unleash Genius by Katie Martin

Unleash Talent: Bringing Out the Best in Yourself and the Learners You Serve by Kara Knollmeyer

Reclaiming Our Calling: Hold On to the Heart, Mind, and Hope of Education by Brad Gustafson

Take the L.E.A.P.: Ignite a Culture of Innovation by Elisabeth Bostwick

Drawn to Teach: An Illustrated Guide to Transforming Your Teaching by Josh Stumpenhorst and illustrated by Trevor Guthke

Math Recess: Playful Learning in an Age of Disruption by Sunil Singh and Dr. Christopher Brownell

Innovate inside the Box: Empowering Learners Through UDL and Innovator's Mindset by George Couros and Katie Novak

Personal & Authentic: Designing Learning Experiences That Last a Lifetime by Thomas C. Murray

Learner-Centered Leadership: A Blueprint for Transformational Change in Learning Communities by Devin Vodicka

Kids These Days: A Game Plan for (Re)Connecting with Those We Teach, Lead, & Love by Dr. Jody Carrington

UDL and Blended Learning: Thriving in Flexible Learning Landscapes by Katie Novak and Catlin Tucker

Teachers These Days: Stories & Strategies for Reconnection by Dr. Jody Carrington and Laurie McIntosh

Because of a Teacher: Stories of the Past to Inspire the Future of Education written and curated by George Couros

Because of a Teacher, Volume 2: Stories from the First Years of Teaching written and curated by George Couros

Evolving Education: Shifting to a Learner-Centered Paradigm by Katie Martin

Adaptable: How to Create an Adaptable Curriculum and Flexible Learning Experiences That Work in Any Environment by A.J. Juliani

Lead from Where You Are: Building Intention, Connection, and Direction in Our Schools by Joe Sanfelippo

The Shift to Student-Led: Reimagining Classroom Workflows with UDL and Blended Learning by Catlin R. Tucker & Katie Novak

The Design Thinking Classroom: Using Design Thinking to Reimagine the Role and Practice of Educators by David Jakes

www.ingramcontent.com/pod-product-compliance
Lightning Source LLC
Chambersburg PA
CBHW050554160426
43199CB00015B/2650